DEATH BY MINIVAN

Heather Anderson Renshaw

Our Sunday Visitor

www.osv.com
Our Sunday Visitor Publishing Division
Our Sunday Visitor, Inc.
Huntington, Indiana 46750

Our Sunday Visitor Publishing Division
Our Sunday Visitor, Inc.
200 Noll Plaza
Huntington, IN 46750
1-800-348-2440

ISBN: 978-1-68192-268-3 (Inventory No. T1958)
eISBN: 978-1-68192-269-0
LCCN: 2018949469

Cover and interior design: Lindsey Riesen
Cover art: Christy Stephens
Interior art: Christy Stephens

PRINTED IN THE UNITED STATES OF AMERICA

"With *Death by Minivan*, Heather Renshaw captures the joys, challenges, and blessings that come with being a mother in the modern world. Her style is relatable. Her humor is infectious. And her love of the Church, the saints, and the Virgin Mary, most evident. I highly recommend this book for all women looking to be affirmed that 'it's all going to be okay' with the guidance of the Most Holy Trinity."

Archbishop Alexander K. Sample,
Archdiocese of Portland in Oregon

"*Death by Minivan* is the mom memoir to end all mom memoirs. No one else needs to write one. Heather Renshaw has done it, and I'm so grateful for it! She's captured what 'mom life' is like (and what we moms can do to become holier) with beautiful honesty, hysterical insights, and the most comforting, relatable tone I've seen in a 'mom book' in ages. I'll be reading this book every year, passing it out to my friends (new and veteran moms alike), and you should grab a copy, too. Buckle up in her minivan's backseat, and enjoy the ride."

— Katie Prejean McGrady, International Catholic
speaker and author of *Room 24: Adventures of a New
Evangelist* and *Follow: Your Lifelong Adventure with Jesus*

"Heather Renshaw gives today's Pinterest-inspired, carefully cropped image of the family a run for its money in her humorous and disarming look at family, faith ... and more family in *Death by Minivan*. She speaks to all of us who have ever sat in pickup lines, coordinated Mass attire on the run, or watched a pot of water not want to boil when trying to get dinner on the table. Heather shares the adventures and challenges of raising a family with joyful, Christ-filled grace in a way that offers hope in this busy season of raising kids."

— Maria Morera Johnson, Author of *My Badass Book of Saints:
Courageous Women Who Showed Me How to Live* and *Super Girls
and Halos: My Companions on the Quest for Truth, Justice, and
Heroic Virtue*

"Heather Renshaw writes with humor and candor to remind us that we're not alone, and we can do this. This book will be a breath of fresh air for any mom who's ever felt like she's failing at her most important job."

— Jennifer Fulwiler, radio host and author of *One Beautiful Dream: The Rollicking Tale of Family Chaos, Personal Passions, and Saying Yes to Them Both*

"Life's path is full of twists, turns, bumps, and blessings. Left to navigate alone, we may break rules, hit gridlock, or even lose our way. Thankfully, *Death by Minivan* reminds us that we never travel alone. With humor, honesty, and spirit, Heather Renshaw employs personal insights and timeless truths to help us harvest the fruits of the Holy Spirit, our companion and GPS along our path to God. Insightful and fun for individuals and even better for group study, this book should be required 'driver training' for busy moms navigating family life."

— Lisa M. Hendey, Founder of CatholicMom.com and author of *The Handbook for Catholic Moms: Nurturing Your Heart, Mind, Body, and Soul*

"Whether you're the mom of one tiny human or a gaggle of kids, *Death by Minivan* will make you laugh, possibly cry, and breathe a big sigh of relief that you're not the only mom out there who seesaws between feeling an intense, visceral love for your children and the very real fear that motherhood will be the end of you—or perhaps your children. Sharing how she's slowly learning to ripen the fruits of the Holy Spirit, Renshaw has written a book that reassures moms they are not alone, while also revealing the grace that can be found in the midst of cold cups of coffee, rogue Legos, what she coins sibling 'bickerpaloozas,' and the calm and the chaos that come with motherhood. Brimming with humor, humility, wisdom from the saints, real-life anecdotes, and biblical encouragement, *Death by Minivan* is like an espresso shot of encouragement for moms everywhere."

— Kate Wicker, speaker and author of *Getting Past Perfect: How to find Joy and Grace in the Messiness of Motherhood* and *Weightless: Making Peace with Your Body*

"As tenderhearted as it is humorous, *Death by Minivan* will manage to give you a good swift kick in the pants, while also encouraging and uplifting you. Well written and worth every word, this book will yield great benefits for the time invested in reading it.

Heather speaks to the heart of every mother who struggles to try harder and be better, and she leads us to a place of peace and genuine happiness. Trade hardness of heart and chaotic inner conversations for the quiet calm of healing and wholeness found by cultivating the fruits of the Holy Spirit."
— Elizabeth Foss, founder and chief content director
of Take Up & Read

"*Death by Minivan* is a raucous joy ride that somehow manages to also be a holy pilgrimage. Heather Renshaw maps a course through life that relies on faith and laughter with the Holy Spirit as your guide. It's breathtaking in places and hilarious in others. Grab your favorite car snacks and settle in for the journey. *Death by Minivan* proves that while motherhood may drive you crazy, it just might be your road to holiness."
— Rebecca Frech, author of *Can We Be Friends* and *Teaching in Your Tiara: A Homeschooling Book for the Rest of Us*, and managing editor for The Catholic Conspiracy website

"Heather Renshaw's book is a beautiful reminder that God is with us every step of the way. Even when life seems crazy and exhausting, he is there pouring out grace and peace. When we look at the frenzy as an opportunity to grow (instead of a chance to cry or whimper!), we will be filled with the virtue God so generously gives. Thank you, Heather, for this fun and sweet reminder that we are not alone and that God wants to pour out every good thing to those who seek him!"
— Rachel Balducci, cohost of *The Gist* on CatholicTV and author of *Raising Boys Is a Full-Contact Sport* and *Make My Life Simple: Bringing Peace to Heart and Home*

"Do you invite Jesus into your chaos? Into the everyday ups and downs of your wild family living, minivan and all? Heather Renshaw does; and luckily, she also invites us along for the ride. Her humor and joy are infectious. Hop on board and you'll find yourself laughing, crying, and commiserating along the way. Heather's gift for storytelling and for seeing the bigger picture will surely bless anyone who reads this book!"
— Danielle Bean, manager at CatholicMom.com

"*Death by Minivan* is a very witty and practical book written by a mom from a mom's perspective; yet it's not just for moms—it's for all of us who have ever felt trapped driving our 'minivans' in this highway called life. This amazing book will help you discover the wisdom of finding God in everything, even in daily routine, through surrender to and acceptance of the movement of the Holy Spirit. So stop for a minute and enjoy a very relatable and deeply spiritual book. You just might drive through life with a different perspective."

— Father Goyo Hidalgo, priest in the Archdiocese
of Los Angeles and associate pastor at Saint Rose of Lima,
Simi Valley, California

*To Ava Madeleine, Elise Gabrielle, Noah James,
Gianna Christine, and Kolbe Joseph —*

*I thank God for each of you—beautifully and wonderfully
made. Stay close to Jesus and Mary and watch what God will
do! I'm so incredibly blessed to be your mother. Love all y'all
to infinity and beyond.*

● ● ●

To David —

*What a long, strange trip it's been! Let's keep going
all the way to heaven, okay? I love you.*

TABLE OF CONTENTS

*"How good God is to give me his
Holy Spirit to supply what I need to strive for
holiness. I must not stray to the right or left, but
keep to the middle of the road—straight as an
arrow—to arrive at a humble detachment from
myself. This will keep me from despair and from
presumption."*

Mother Angelica

• • •

*"If evolution really works,
how come mothers only have two hands?"*

Milton Berle

FOREWORD

• • •

Heather Renshaw and I share a love for cold Long Island iced teas and bad karaoke. As a matter of fact, it's how we met in the summer of 2015 in Charleston, South Carolina. We were both attending the Edel Gathering hosted by the phenomenal Jennifer Fulwiler and Hallie Lord, and a karaoke dance party with two hundred of our closest girlfriends was the highlight of the event. Two things you need to know: I was a high school choir dropout, and one of Heather's love languages is musical theater.

I sang "All About That Bass" by Meghan Trainor and sounded like a drowned cat. Heather took the stage and belted out, in perfect pitch mind you, "RESPECT" by Aretha Franklin. She took us to church, and it was glorious. It takes quite a bit of *chutzpah* to get two hundred women to sing along, but Heather, she's got *chutzpah* in spades. She is sassy, funny, a tad snarky, but full of the Holy Spirit. We became immediate friends, and my life has been forever changed in the very best of ways.

Over the last three years we have walked through many challenges together, as God has stretched our faith and grown our friendship. Heather's encouraging words always land gently, even when they reveal a hidden truth about something that may need rooting out or changing. We're both passionate about women's ministry and lifting up those who feel marginalized and unseen.

When Heather enters your world, it gets brighter, funnier, and more exciting. Your heart is filled with the sure confidence and peace that you will not be abandoned on the side of the road. Heather is your roadside assistance plan, and she is darn good at it. She sees your heart and speaks with truth and grace. She encourages and uplifts while walking alongside you, holding you up when you cannot stand on your own. She is a woman of God on a mission to make sure you know that as woman, wife, sister, and mother, you are seen, known, and loved by a God who has drawn a very unique and special road map just for you to follow.

Heather is one heck of a travel buddy. Imagine those minivan windows rolled down, wind whipping your hair, hands in the air, while the Fresh Prince and DJ Jazzy Jeff accompany you down the highway of life.

Death by Minivan is a celebration of motherhood with all its twists and turns along those mountain roads you are terrified to navigate. Using the fruits of the Holy Spirit as a guide to celebrate seeing motherhood as God's carefully considered gift to us for our sanctification, Heather shares the truth of God's economy of embracing our cross to be free, dying to live, giving to receive.

Some of us love the ups and downs of hills and valleys, some prefer the winding mountain road, and others the straight and narrow surrounded by wheat fields as far as the eye can see. No matter your landscape preference, no matter your past driving record or how many speeding tickets or fender benders you have been involved in, every woman's road map is unique to her and the passengers whom God has created to fill her minivan along the way.

This book you are holding is filled with inspiration and encouragement as Heather shares her heart, freely and fully, so that you might not feel alone on your own journey. Her experience is vast and varied. Her love for Christ, her husband, and their five blessings resonates throughout each page. They are her true north, her guiding lights. The stories shared within just might inspire you to step outside your comfort zone and trust a little more in the plan God has for you and your family.

No one travels the same road in the same way. There will be roadblocks—and many of them. But don't be afraid of them or the occasional flat tire from the construction debris on the side of the road. Trust in the GPS that the Holy Spirit provides and listen closely for the sirens of the emergency vehicles that will arrive just in time to save the day.

Dig in, friends, and savor this book. Celebrate the sacrificial yet fruitful call to love and allow it to change your perspective on motherhood. Now crank up the radio, and let's get this road trip started. Life is a highway, and all roads lead to heaven.

Mary Lenaburg
author, writer, and speaker
www.marylenaburg.com

MAMAS,
START YOUR ENGINES

((and now an introductory word or two from our author))

*"Most of the time, I feel entirely unqualified to be a parent.
I call these times being awake."*

— *Jim Gaffigan*

• • •

This whole written journey through the mother'hood began because I was up-to-my-eyeballs frustrated.

Mile after mile, hour after hour, day after seemingly endless day, I transported my beloved children in our beat-up minivan to destinations both hither and yon and back again. It was a thankless, mind-numbing task. And pretty numbing of other body parts, too, come to think of it.

I felt trapped in a ridiculously sensible vehicle with freakishly loud short people who neither appreciated my music playlist nor my air-conditioning needs. It was also only a matter of time before I completely lost my sense of hearing due to the sheer volume of noise assaulting my eardrums from the back seat.

Perhaps most telling about my pit-of-despair mindset was this: I just knew I had more important things to do with my time than lugging children around—even children I deeply and fiercely loved. Because, after all, I didn't aspire to be a chauffeur (or a maid, or a short-order cook, or a nanny) when I grew up, so why was I relegated to all these tasks (and more) without so much as a paycheck to show for it?

My minivan had become a metaphor—a visible sign that I'd lost the last vestiges of my youth, my potential for cool, and my hard-fought independence. It represented everything I'd given up so my children could have what (and get to where) they needed.

The minivan represented eventual, total, and complete annihilation: death. And perhaps even scarier: *carpooling.*

Now, while I would much prefer death by *chocolate,* or *spa day,* or countless other pleasant things, that's not where God has me.

In my heart of hearts, I know that family life is where God wants me, for better or worse. This is my vocation, my calling, my path to holiness. And so, I determined with a bullheaded willfulness known to my confessor alone that I would, with God's grace and quite a bit of caffeine, endeavor to despise my minivan and the countless sacrifices it represented slightly less today than I had yesterday.

Besides, maybe if I tried harder to accept the road map I'd been given for this crazy adventure called life, I'd only be significantly wounded rather than outright killed by my minivan metaphor. Hey—a girl can dream, right?

Eventually, I conceded that death is inevitable; it doesn't discriminate. As Sister Theresa Aletheia often reminds her Twitter followers: #mementomori (remember your death). Perhaps, though, my sacrifice—my dying to self—could accomplish something, like in John 12:24, where he wrote, "Unless a grain of wheat falls into the earth and dies, it remains alone; but if it dies, it bears much fruit."

I wondered: what sort of fruit could I bear by laying down my life for my husband and children? I remembered a choral piece I sang in church choir before we had kids. Its lyrics were based on Galatians 5:22-23: "The fruit of the Spirit is love, joy, peace, patience, kindness, goodness, faithfulness, gentleness, and self-control. If you walk in the Spirit, let your life reflect the fruit of God's love."

There. *That! That* was the sort of woman—the sort of mother—I wanted to be! I wanted to be more loving, joyful, peaceful, patient, gentle, and all the rest. *I wanted to walk by the Spirit!*

But how? That was the million-dollar question.

I don't know about you, but I figure things out by talking and writing about them, so I started doing just that.

I wrote about the realities of mom life—how we sacrifice brain cells, energy, clean clothes, and washed hair for our kids, but how, even with all of that, a plethora of good fruit can be harvested, up to and including eternity spent with God in heaven.

Answering God's call to unconditionally love our spouse and our children—traveling the straight and narrow way—takes a lot of practice. It takes sacrifice. And it takes many, many acts of the will that are often contrary to our impulses and feelings. If we want to live by the Spirit, we have to intentionally and consistently choose to incorporate good, godly fruits into our busy lives.

We moms, I figured, often give of ourselves until there's not much left to give. Basically, we're dying to ourselves for the good of our families all the time already. Couldn't we possibly enjoy some tantalizing fruit as partial payment for our efforts along the way?

Now, I know what you're thinking: *Heather, this sort of sounds like the worst road trip EVER!! I'm gonna die, and you want me to settle for some fruit as a consolation prize?* The certain reality is, none of us is going to make it off this highway called life alive, but we can praise and glorify God with the windows rolled down and the music turned up while we are able, so ... why not?

It took me quite some time, but I now know that the very best place for me to learn about receiving and giving God's love is ... yep! in my metaphorical (and actual) minivan, backing out of the garage on the "x" that marks the spot where my very own family may be found.

It's in the small, hidden ways (and the big, loud ones, too) that God is directing and leading ever closer to my final destination.

This book truly is a love letter for you, mamas-in-arms! I sure hope you like it and find it somewhat helpful.

You oughta know

The first fruit of the Holy Spirit is love, and that's exactly what kept my engine revved as I wrote this book for you—yes, you! *Death by Minivan* is my love letter to you and every other mama heading into, smack dab in the middle of, or heading out of the trenches of the mother'hood.

Here's what I hope you'll get out of it:

- I want you to know that you are not tackling the towering mountains of diapers and laundry and schoolwork and snacks and fevers and playdates and dust bunnies and doctor appointments and wet kisses and boo-boos and grocery lists and teen talk and cooking by yourself. There are countless sisters out there just like you, who are also striving toward holiness one milepost at a time. He's got a plan for you, and you aren't alone. We've almost got a carpool going on up in here!

- I want you to know that you are enough, just as you are, and you can most assuredly handle this crazy, grace-filled journey called motherhood, because God can and will provide every grace and blessing that you need through the power of the Holy Spirit for you to bear abundant fruit.

- I want you to know that it is okay if you do things differently than other moms. The world needs some of your unique flavor and spice, and it needs your kids' individuality, too. Embrace the kind of mama God created you to be and watch the road start to get a bit smoother, sweeter, and more fruitful.

- I want you to know that, even if you might think you're messing up this whole motherhood gig, it's okay, because God alone is perfect. If you're like me, you'd start a savings plan for your kids' future therapy needs—if you could afford it. Yet no matter how inadequate you may feel, God is good. He's faithful. He's got this. He has you, your husband, and your kids, every mountain you'll ever have to scale, every valley you'll ever wander.

- I want you to know how very, very much you are loved. Right here, right now. In the messiness, in the joys, in the struggles, in the blessings, in the brokenness. How you are loved big by an even bigger God. And how "loved big" is an epic understatement. How he can handle all your joys, sorrows, frustrations, and celebrations. He's in this with you for the long haul, because he knows the path you're traveling is difficult, but so very worth it. You were worth his journey to Calvary two thousand years ago, and you're worth accompanying on the winding roads that make up your life today.

This book exists because I thought you might need to hear these things every once in a while, just like I do.

Now you should know upfront that just because I have five kids doesn't mean I'm a parenting expert or a better mom than you. No way, no how! And just because I write about spiritual things doesn't mean I'm a theologian or a biblical scholar. I'm a Christian mom faithful to the Church who has (mostly!) surrendered herself and her husband and children to the merciful arms of Jesus Christ, hoping that we all reach our final destination (heaven) someday.

To be clear, this book is not meant to be a how-to manual, because even after sixteen years in the mother'hood, *I* don't always know exactly "how to"! Plus, *your* "how to" for life with your family will likely look different from mine, and that's absolutely okay.

God willing, this book will inject some encouragement, commiseration, inspiration, and bursts of laughter into your life. Amen, alleluia, and praise God!

How to win at reading this book

Each chapter focuses on one of the fruits of the Holy Spirit found in Galatians, along with the four other nontraditional fruits I added. I began by reflecting on how that chapter's fruit applies to our lives. Some chapters also include specific roadblocks or practical ideas for cultivating a particular fruit. Each chapter contains some helpful components for further reflection, discussion, and prayer, including:

- *Yield to the power of the Holy Spirit.* A brief prayer to the Holy Spirit for the specific fruit at the end of the chapter.

- *GPS: God Positioning System.* Scripture verses to illuminate your reading. Perfect for prayer, meditation, and possible memorization (#goals).

- *Roadside Assistance.* Selected excerpts from the saints and others are included to inspire and provoke (in a good way).

- *Pit Stop.* Various other resources or suggestions are listed to help you on your journey. Take what works for you and leave what doesn't! There's also space for you to include your own ideas.

- *Discuss Amongst Yourselves.* In case you decide to read this book with other moms, I've added discussion questions at the end of each chapter to spark personal reflection and more in-depth conversation.

So, my friend: read this book alone, in your favorite chair or your favorite coffee shop. Or in the park. Or at the library. Or in the pickup line. Or the drive-through. Or in the bathroom (I won't tell). Rip apart my theories and conclusions. Come up with your own. Take a nap if you can. Read some more.

Or read it with your friends. Listen to one other. Have something to drink. Laugh a lot! Pray together. Be sisters in Christ. This book was written *for you* under the influence of my children. Now you can't say I didn't warn you.

Mamas, start your engines!

BUCKLE UP, BUTTERCUP

((prologue))

• • •

"Ummm … " I stammered, "am I supposed to feel like I'm driving my living room around on the road?"

My sweaty hands gripped the steering wheel as I attempted to navigate a lane change. I'd never been so grateful for seatbelts and airbags in my life. The car salesman chuckled from the passenger seat next to me. "It takes a little bit of getting used to, but consider all the space you'll have!"

"Isn't this great, Babe? All this space!" my husband enthused from the backseat.

"Yeah!" I responded through lips forced into a faker-than-fake smile. "*Great!*"

Space. I couldn't deny that it was at a premium these days. After spending several enjoyable months as the proud owners of an attractive, mid-sized SUV, we realized that, once the new baby arrived (our fourth), we'd need more room for yet another car seat, as well as the additional 3,267 things tiny humans need to stay alive.

I let out a weighty sigh, trying to focus my attention on the road, but I couldn't help wondering how we'd gotten here. To clarify: I knew exactly *how* we became parents of three small children with another on the way; after all, our sweet babies didn't just magically appear in my uterus. What I was having a hard time wrapping my brain around was how we had, seemingly overnight, become—*bum bum buuummmmm*—People Who Needed A Minivan.

How could we let this happen?

Okay, so I know how we "let" "this" "happen." Because of love and marriage and God and openness to life (because them's the rules) and a miracle and two pink lines. That's how. Necessity is a mother, and once I found out I was pregnant, I was necessarily a mom. End of story. And I honestly thought that I had come to terms with that. Well, mostly. Yet, here I was, lamenting the purchase of an announcement on wheels: "HERE COMES A MOM WITH A BUNCH OF KIDS!"

In my mind, *fun* people did not drive minivans. *Cool* people did not drive minivans. Surely accomplished, motivated women who did amazing things beyond shuttling children to and fro did not drive minivans. At least, I didn't think they did. And yet, here I was. Driving a minivan.

Now, some of you may be thinking, "What's the big flipping deal? It's a *minivan*, for crying out loud, not the end of the world. You're lucky you could afford to buy what your family needed!"

And you're absolutely right. We were very blessed to qualify for a loan on a used vehicle in good condition. And you're also correct to point out that buying a minivan is not the end of the actual world. I would counter, however, that purchasing a colossal-sized family room on wheels symbolized the end of *a* world—one in which I imagined cruising the streets at dusk, warm wind kissing my cheeks and bass bumping from my custom stereo as my manageable number of children quietly played travel games together with the windows of our not-too-big family vehicle rolled down. Succumbing to Minivan World somehow meant enveloping myself in an inescapable chamber of screaming and bickering, with a soundtrack of saccharine-sweet kiddie tunes reverberating off the walls, because certain short people couldn't keep their body parts inside when the windows were cracked.

I just wanted a decent, culturally acceptable rig that wouldn't make me self-conscious. One that I could park in one of those spots with a "C" (for "compact") on it. One that didn't smell of petrified French fries, sweaty feet, and despairing cleaning products. One that didn't smell like broken dreams.

In my mind, buying this minivan meant my husband and I (but especially me, since I would be driving the darn thing) had finally given up trying to have an identity outside of family life. We'd hoisted the white flag, thrown in the towel, and thrown up a little in our mouths. Because, really? What was left after this but even more children, even more sleepless nights, even more worry about how to pay the bills, and eventually … gasp … a *full-sized van*. Buying this vehicle truly symbolized the absolute end of the world according to Heather. Again.

See, I hadn't always been a somewhat neurotic practicing Catholic mother of a few, going on more, striving for holiness despite my many faults and failings. I once was a neurotic non-practicing Catholic who wanted to live my life by my rules, according to my passions and desires. I was living in the world according to Heather.

In the 1990s, Tom Cochrane sang about how "Life is a Highway." He wasn't wrong. What he couldn't have known, though, is that not too many years after that song was a big hit, I'd decided to travel down a highway of my own design. I'd chucked the map my parents gave me. I ignored the signposts provided by the Faith into which I was baptized as an infant. I started making bad turn after bad turn and eventually became hopelessly lost. I missed the mile markers and the dashboard lights God kept sending to get my attention. Eventually, he resorted to billboards.

Finally, with my tank completely depleted and more dings and crunches on my soul than I cared to admit, I coasted to the shoulder, feeling like a defeated pile of junk. It was then that I realized I had to call in some spiritual "Triple-A"—Almighty Amen + Alleluia—Roadside Assistance to get me off this crazy, hell-bound path and back on to the highway toward heaven. It was time to make a U-turn.

And so I did. Through God's grace and infinite mercy, I was the prodigal returning home to the Father. I began going to Mass again. I began receiving the sacraments again. I really dove into my faith, trying to understand what I'd missed in my CCD classes growing up (which, unfortunately, was a lot). I married a Catholic, just like my mom always told me to do. I'd set aside much of my previous sinful behavior and was following the narrow way. I'd given up the world according to Heather to try to live in the World According to the Savior. Yet it seemed like my heavenly Father wasn't content just to refurbish the parts of me that showed on the outside; there was an immense amount of detail work that needed to be done on the inside as well. God wanted a complete overhaul of my soul.

We've all heard the phrase, "Bloom where you're planted," right? Yeah, that wasn't really my thing back in my early parenting days. Listening, waiting, patience? Not really my bag, either. Self-control, peace, gentleness … let's just say it turns out I was not naturally inclined toward much that leads to holiness. Even after my reversion to the Faith, even after being married in the Church and being open to life, even after The Great Minivan Purchase of aught-eight, I was prone to act before thinking, speak before listening, and complain before thanking. I overlooked grace-filled moments and, frankly, didn't enjoy my life as a mom all that much. I thought that to be holy I had to be a quiet, serious, minivan-driving mama who just accepted that life was a lot of meaningless pain, suffering, and non-fun. Sadly, I was an exponentially messier mess than I am today, and likely a stumbling block for myself and others, including my children.

I still had a very long way to go.

I'll never forget when I first heard that we are *all* called to sainthood—every last one of us—and that we cannot be in heaven unless we are saints. I figured that was my cue to pack up my stuff and peel out of the parking lot. Because, seriously? The impulsive, impatient, perfectionistic, self-defeating person in the mirror? Saint Heather? Don't make me spit out my coconut milk latte all over the steering wheel!

But none other than one of my spiritual heroes, the plucky and devout Mother Angelica, foundress of the Eternal Word Television Network (EWTN), dropped this truth bomb, and it struck me square between the eyes: "Holiness is not for wimps, and the Cross is not negotiable, sweetheart. It's a requirement." *Woah.*

I figured that what I lacked in holiness, I more than made up for in stubbornness and grit, thanks be to God, genetics, and environmental conditioning. I kept at it—looking for the loophole that would save a wretch like me, something that would push me over the finish line and through the pearly gates. I did a lot of praying and thinking, sometimes as I nursed babies, sometimes in my minivan, and sometimes as I wept from sheer exhaustion. What was the meaning of all this relentless offering up of my body, mind, and soul, I wondered?

Over time, I finally began to realize that, yes, even *I* could be a saint, and that I didn't have to completely reject my personality, talents, desires, and dreams to do it. *I just had to take up my cross and follow Jesus.*

God wanted to do something good with this "dying to self" business that was happening whenever I was broken and offered it up for my family (which, frankly, was quite often). The day we bought the minivan was just another tip on yet another iceberg, another beginning of the beginning. He didn't just want to work the obvious good of making it possible to fit all our kids and their stuff and the groceries into one rig. No, his dream for me was much deeper, wider, and grander than I could initially see or imagine.

God wanted me to be a new creation in Christ, emptied of self and sinfulness so he could fill me to the brim with his abiding love. In turn, I would be able to pour God's love out to my husband, our children, our community, and beyond. He was showing me that he was going to use this minivan, and everything it represented—and, probably more accurately, its inhabitants—to cultivate the fruits of the Holy

Spirit in my life. Indeed, the single grain of wheat that was my life, fallen to the ground and dying through the sacrifices of everyday life in the mother'hood, could actually yield a fruitful and bountiful harvest.

He was telling me that I already had the map to becoming the sort of mom I wanted to be: loving, peaceful, joyful, kind, gentle, faithful, good, self-controlled, patient, forgiving, humble, grateful, and, yes, a little bit funny. And here was the secret: that same map could also, God willing, lead me and all my backseat riders straight to our ultimate destination: Heaven.

FILL 'ER UP

((love))

"There really are places in the heart you
don't even know exist until you love a child."

— Anne Lamott

● ● ●

I used to think love was all about good feelings, but then my six-month-old threw up on me.

Now, this wasn't just run-of-the-mill infant spit-up, mind you. This was completely out-of-the-blue, large-volume, straight-to-the-face, down-the-shirt, into-the-bra, real person *puke*.

I think we were both a little shocked. I looked at my daughter, and she looked at me. I'm not sure if it was the act of vomiting for the first time that upset her, or the horrified look on my face, but she began to cry. In that moment, I was simultaneously repulsed beyond belief yet filled with overwhelming compassion for this poor, helpless kid. I pulled her closer to me, saying, "It's okay, sweetheart. Mama's here. You're okay," while five-alarm sirens blared in my head, shrieking: "RUNN AWAAAAY! SAVE YOURSELLLLF! THE END IS NIIIIIGHHH!"

After a bit, she calmed down, and then we did the next loving thing: we hopped in the shower for a good, long while.

And I could be wrong, but I like to think that my heart grew three sizes that day, sorta like the Grinch of Seussian lore. I was beginning to understand what real love looked like. It wasn't always pretty, but it was persistent.

There was no question that I loved my husband—enough to enter into a covenant relationship in front of God and the priest and my parents and everybody. But when Ava Madeleine was born, it was like the faucet that regulated my capacity to love was cranked up to full blast, until it reached geyser level. I didn't even know this kid well yet, but I had the distinct understanding that I would literally throw myself in front of a truck to keep her safe. This was new territory for me.

Comedian and writer Amy Poehler said of motherhood: "I love my boys so much I fear my heart will explode. I wonder if this love will crack open my chest and split me in half. It is scary, this love."

And she's right. It *can* be scary. But, at least in my case, so was driving for the first time. And the first day of school. And my first date. And having someone calling me "Mom." Scary, but also exciting. What I've found is that, if we ask, the Holy Spirit will equip us with the strength and courage we need to accomplish whatever we need to do according to his will, including hugging little girls (and/or boys) who just puked all over us.

No greater love has a mom …

Maybe you've heard this saying: if you want to know what real love is, look at a crucifix. I've heard it, too, and I remain humbled and eternally grateful that the Creator of the universe loved me enough to die. What I didn't know was that it would be through my calling as a wife and mother that I would truly understand what it meant to die to myself for the sake of another—for the sake of love.

A funny thing happens when you begin traveling this road to holiness called motherhood: lots of things change. At least, they did for me.

Suddenly, I was thinking about someone else's needs as more important than my own. Did the baby get enough to eat? How many wet diapers has she had? Did we forget her blankie? *Is she breathing??* Meanwhile, I wasn't really eating so well myself, or going to the bathroom on my own, or remembering my name or what day it was due to severe sleep deprivation. For the record, I do NOT recommend this model of postpartum recovery, as it's completely ridiculous and totally unsustainable. If you want to know how to really do it right, search online for "how to postpartum like a boss" and see what my friend Blythe had to say about it over at her blog, *The Fike Life*. I promise you'll thank me (but especially Blythe).

Anyway, it wasn't as if I'd never put others' needs before mine, of course, but this was exponentially different. This little baby girl needed *so very much* from me at all times and couldn't do a thing (save the occasional gas bubble I decided to believe was a smile) to repay me for my efforts.

And the crazy thing was, other than wishing I could actually sleep for a few hours in a row, go to the bathroom in peace, and fit into my pre-pregnancy *anything*, I was okay with it. Glad, even! What a miracle! What a blessing! My husband and I had created, with God's help, another human being! We were totally, thoroughly, head-over-heels in love. We were also totally, thoroughly, orange-juice-poured-into-the-cereal bowl exhausted.

It wasn't long before I wondered whether I would ever feel like a real human being again.

Over the years, I've heard a lot of talk around the concept of the "Martyr Mom." You know—a well-meaning friend tells another friend, "Don't be a martyr!" And what she means is, "Quit sacrificing your mental, physical, and spiritual health on the altar of perfectionistic, Pinterest-worthy motherhood!" For the record: I agree 100 percent. I am fully and completely on board with moms taking care of themselves. And I mean that from the bottom of my heart. Love your kiddos and your husband and your neighbors as you love yourself. I encourage all mothers everywhere to do what they need to do to soak up God's love whenever and however they can. I do *not* advocate taking on more than you can handle, because I've been there, and it is *not* a good road to travel. It leads to much crash, lots burn.

What I'm suggesting is this: sacrificing our own wants and desires for the good of our children in motherhood is bound to happen, whether we're ready for it or not. It's kind of part of the job description. So, how about we moms decide to reclaim the word "martyr" and restore it to its original glory? A martyr is someone who dies—whether physically or in a spiritual sense—for his or her Christian faith. But the word martyr doesn't mean "dead." It means "witness." A martyr is one who bears witness to the Gospel. As mothers, we are frontline witnesses. We bear witness to Jesus Christ in our children's lives; we bear witness to other moms, encouraging one another in our common sisterhood; we bear witness to God's strength, glory, and power, even if we can't see it sometimes through the muck and the mire of everyday living. We moms can bear witness to our faith precisely *through* our calling to motherhood, every time we die to ourselves by performing acts of love for our very own "least of these"—our children.

Call me an out-of-touch throwback, but if we're using this reclaimed definition of "martyr," I'm in. I want to be a martyr. I want to be a witness. I want to be someone whose life testifies to the love of God in my marriage and in my motherhood. It would be ludicrous to think I can do it on my own, broken, weak, and sinful as I am. But if I allow Jesus to take the wheel of my heart, and the Holy Spirit to be the motor animating my actions? Hallelujah! I wonder what a witness I could be.

Yes, Mom, I was listening

Growing up, my parents frequently told me, "Love is not a feeling—it's a decision." And when I say "frequently," I mean I heard it about a *million* times. And yet, even into my newlywed years, the concept of human love being anything more than good feelings flew right over my head. In all those years, I must have done *something* because of love rather than duty, guilt, shame, or what I'd get out of it, but I still didn't understand that love was a choice that I could make.

Until I was a mom.

They say the longest distance in the world is the ten inches from the head to the heart, and that certainly rings true. In my case, however, covering that distance took precisely 21 ¾ inches and a little more than nine pounds of baby.

Let's take a slight detour here for a moment. How much did you know about driving a car, really, before you sat behind the wheel? If you were like me, prior to taking the test for your driver's permit, you probably read the manual. You might even have studied it. And hopefully you passed. For me, it wasn't until I actually had my hands at ten and two on the steering wheel (that's how we did it when I was a kid) and my foot hovering over the gas pedal with my dad riding shotgun that it hit me: "Wow. This is a big deal. I better take this seriously." In other words, it was personal. I was calling the shots. I was accelerating and braking and turning and avoiding potholes and pedestrians. If I ever wanted to pass the driving test and get my license, I was going to have to demonstrate that I was a competent driver. And I learned to drive by … driving. I practiced. My dad was my coach from the passenger seat, but I was the one behind the wheel. I had to choose to do it.

Now, as the mom of a teen itching to get her driver's permit, the thought of fifteen-year-olds cruising around on the highways and byways scares the poop out of me. I don't think I'm alone in my anxiety.

Here's the point: To genuinely show love to those around us, we have to practice being loving to them—not just in our words, but in our actions, too. Those fizzy, fluttery, twitter-pated, lovey-dovey feelings may be MIA, but we can *choose* to do the next loving thing anyway. And I've been around the block enough times to know that it's tough to flip a U-turn with my behavior when my thoughts are angry, unkind, and resentful. I have to choose to shore up my thoughts so that they're loving, too.

It sounds like an awful lot of work, doesn't it?

Except, here's an often overlooked reality: *You're already doing it.*

You're already doing the work of being loving, my friend. Every mom knows exactly what it's like to sacrifice her own body; brain cells; schedule; short-, mid-, and long-term plans; and personal hygiene for the sake of her kids. The question is: are you doing the work, making the sacrifices, offering it up … with *love*? BOY-YOY-YOY-YOING!! That's the sound of me being convicted by my own words. Every day, I have to ask myself: am I doing small things (and big things, too—have you *seen* my laundry pile?) with great love, as Saint Thérèse of Lisieux said, or am I complaining about the cooking (gah), the dishes (oy), the clutter (gak), the driving (oh, my word), the children's sass (!!) and all of the 9,432,681 things that come with being a mom?

I'll always remember when I realized what a noisy gong and a clanging cymbal I tend to be about certain tasks. It turns out that I *can* get all the laundry washed, folded, hung up, and put away, but if I'm not doing it with love, I'm missing the point. I can master meal-scheduling, crush grocery-shopping, successfully herd everyone out the door, get them where the need to be on time, and slay my to-do list … but if I don't have love, what is the point? (See 1 Corinthians 13:1–3.)

Eventually, I asked myself: what would happen if I just did these small (and big) things with as much love as my overwhelmed, overworked, overtired, overstimulated mind, body, and soul could muster? Wouldn't that make a much more pleasing sacrifice to God than if I grumbled the whole time? I thought of the widow in Mark's Gospel (see 12:41–44), who only had two copper coins to give. That totaled—wait for it—a penny. And yet Jesus said her offering was worth more than what everyone else gave to the treasury, because she gave everything she had, not just a little bit from the extra she had left. Depending on the day and circumstances, I'm not sure I have even half a coin's worth to give! But if I am only able to offer that half coin, if I can choose to give it with love, God is very pleased with my offering.

Let God love on you

Speaking of God being pleased, do you know how much God loves you? I know, I know. Maybe this sounds cheesy and makes you really uncomfortable, but please hear me out.

Think about the one person who loves you the very most out of every other human being on this entire planet. This person is your "ride or die"—the one who, no questions asked, will rush to fill up your tank whenever you need it. Through good times and bad, they love you. Maybe this person is your husband, or your sister, or your best friend, or your own mother. If you have someone like this in your life, thank God for them! I pray you get to do life with this person every single day and twice on Sunday, or at least on a regular basis.

Some of us don't have the blessing of a "ride or die" person in our lives, and that's okay. Don't lose heart! Keep praying that Mama Mary and Elizabeth of the Visitation will send you this kind of friend; I will pray for that, too! I'm thinking, though, that if you're reading this book, you have one or more children in your life, or you hope to someday.

So … think about that child or those children. Consider how much you love them. How you'd do anything for them. How you sacrifice so much, so that they can have the kind of life you want them to have. How you worry when something's wrong. How you celebrate when things go right. How you pray. How you hope. And pray some more. Think about how very much you love the children in your life.

But here's the thing: we could combine all the love your ride or die has for you with how much love you have for your kids, add that to the love shared between each and every other person on our planet, and it would *still* be a substantially weak approximation of the love your heavenly Father has for you. Just you. Not the entire human race—*you*.

Because God's love for you is infinite. Lavish. Extravagant. Beyond human comprehension. Before he formed you in the womb he knew you (see Jer 1:5). And he knows you still. He wants you. He'll never turn his back on you, not ever. Because he loves you.

And he's not a loophole lover, this God. He isn't waiting for you to make a wrong turn, or miss your exit, or run out of gas so he can stop being burdened by loving you. Nope. No way, no how. His love for you is infinite, and it is unconditional. You are his beloved child, his precious daughter. You cannot do anything to earn or to lose his love. It just *is*.

Now consider not just loving your child, but sacrificing that child to save others. That would take a super huge love; some might even call it supernatural. And yet this is the immense love God shows for us—that even while we were still sinners, he sent his Son, Jesus, to die for us so that we might live (see Rom 5:8).

It's actually sort of mind-blowing to consider how much he loves us.

Knowing how much God loves me motivates me. It guides and directs me. It helps me to continue to pour myself out for my family day in and day out, when I feel I don't have anything left to give. I look to the sacrificial love of Jesus Christ, and I see how my path to holiness—my vocation— echoes the ultimate sacrifice of Calvary. I also see my future. Not necessarily with literal death on a cross, but with the beautiful resurrection that awaits those whose lives most resembled Christ's on this earth—the resurrection of the body and life everlasting. My life, your life, our children's lives.

My friend, it is my greatest hope that you may acknowledge, accept, and be permeated with and re-created by God's lavish and unfathomable love for you. I pray that it fills you up to overflowing, binding your wounds and fueling your days. I pray that, because you choose to allow God's love to dwell within you, that you are, in turn, able to be his love to your family, your community, yourself.

I don't have to tell you that sometimes love smells pretty bad. Sometimes it's reallllly messy. And sometimes it's just plain uncomfortable. But, as Pope Emeritus Benedict XVI said, we are not called to comfort. Mama, we are called to *greatness.* And if we choose to do small things with great love, we can navigate this crazy trip called motherhood, one overdue math assignment, one broken teen heart, one impromptu jump into the shower at a time.

● ● ●

Roadblocks to love

Here are a few common roadblocks we might experience on our journey to love.

Unworthiness: I think everyone believes, at one time or another for whatever reason, that they aren't worthy of love. Well, we're going to send that lie straight back to the pit of hell from whence it came! In Jeremiah 31:3, the Lord says, "I have loved you with an everlasting love." You. Love. Everlasting. Sit with that truth. Soak it in. Believe it. He sent his Son to die for *you.* Before you were in your mother's womb he *knew* you. You *are* lovable and you are *loved.* End of story.

Wounds: Maybe you've allowed yourself the exquisite joy of loving another person with everything you've got, only to be crushed when that love wasn't reciprocated. Or it was betrayed. Or taken advantage of. Or discarded out of hand. I'm so very sorry you were hurt in that way! Here's the good news: unconditional love *is* possible, because God loves us without condition and God is *real.* The Divine Physician wants to bind up your wounds and make you whole again, able to receive his abundant love until your heart overflows.

Don't allow fear to keep you from experiencing the greatest love of all—God's love for you.

Selfishness (personal agenda/selfish desires): Sometimes we can get caught up in the "what's in it for me" mentality regarding relationships. We don't want to give love unless we know we'll get something in return. But that's not what God calls us to. He calls us to lay down our lives, to love as he loves, even those who hate us. The Holy Spirit can help us purify our desires and foster a more unconditional, self-giving love if we ask him to. So, let's ask.

• • •

Yield to the power of the Holy Spirit
(prayer)

Eternal God, in whom mercy is endless and the treasury of compassion inexhaustible, look kindly upon us and increase your mercy in us, that in difficult moments we might not despair nor become despondent, but with great confidence submit ourselves to your holy will, which is love and mercy itself. *(Closing prayer from the Chaplet of Divine Mercy)*

Come, Holy Spirit—fill me with your love. Amen.

• • •

GPS: God Positioning System
(scripture)

"Greater love has no man than this, that a man lay down his life for his friends." — John 15:13

"For God so loved the world that he gave his only Son, that whoever believes in him should not perish but have eternal life." — John 3:16

"Let all that you do be done in love." — 1 Corinthians 16:14

"Through love be servants of one another."
— Galatians 5:13

• • •

Roadside Assistance

(wisdom from the saints and others)

"God loves each of us as if there were only one of us."
— Saint Augustine of Hippo

"Sometimes my worst day—one filled with pain and suffering—in the eyes of God, is my best day if I've borne it cheerfully and I've borne it with love."
— Mother Angelica

"Let us remember that love lives through sacrifice and is nourished by giving. Without sacrifice, there is no love."
— Saint Maximilian Kolbe

"Love, to be real, it must cost—it must hurt—it must empty us of self." — Saint Teresa of Calcutta

"Accustom yourself continually to make many acts of love, for they enkindle and melt the soul."
— Saint Teresa of Ávila

"When you know how much God is in love with you, then you can only live your life radiating that love."
— Saint Teresa of Calcutta

• • •

Pit Stop

(other resources)

- Look up 1 Corinthians 13, the well-known New Testament passage on love. Copy down or read aloud the passage, beginning with verse 1 and ending with "love never ends" in verse 8. Substitute the name of God everywhere the word "love" is referenced. Quietly meditate upon the true nature of God, who *is* love.

- Next, change things up, inserting your own name wherever the word "love" is referenced, beginning with verse 4 and ending with verse 6 (that is, "Heather is patient and kind; Heather is not jealous or boastful," etc.). Meditate upon this modified version of the Scripture passage, especially as it relates to your vocation as a mother.

- Look up the song "You are Mine" by David Haas. Imagine God is speaking directly to you through the lyrics. If you're a visual or audio person, there are videos with lyrics and music you can watch or listen to online.

- We all want to love and be loved. Perhaps you've read *The 5 Love Languages* by Gary Chapman. There's also a children's version, appropriately called *The 5 Love Languages of Children*. I've found these books, along with some free online resources, to be very helpful in understanding how I, my husband, and our children show and receive love. I encourage you to check them out!

● ● ●

Your Ideas

_____

_____

_____

_____

_____

_____

_____

● ● ●

Discuss Amongst Yourselves
(questions)

1. What is unconditional love? How do you practice this particular love in your home?

2. What does it mean to be "fearfully and wonderfully made," as Scripture tells us in Psalms 139:14?

3. Consider a time when your best-laid plans took a back seat to the needs of your child or children. What were the circumstances? What was the result of your sacrifice?

4. What are two things you can do this week to allow God's love to be poured into you? Into your children?

WINDOWS ROLLED DOWN, MUSIC CRANKED UP

((joy))

"My mother is a big believer in being responsible for your own happiness. She always talked about finding joy in small moments and insisted that we stop and take in the beauty of an ordinary day. When I stop the car to make my kids really see a sunset, I hear my mother's voice and smile."

— Jennifer Garner

● ● ●

It's 7:55 in the morning. The teenager missed her ride to school because she's having a breakdown about moisturizer and schoolwork. The six-year-old refuses to return the earbuds she swiped from the twelve-year-old, who is protesting the injustice at the top of her lungs. The preschooler woke up late, and I'm scrambling to get him and myself fed, dressed, and out the door while the nine-year-old waits impatiently in the garage, wondering what all the fuss is about.

In this moment, I am *not* a happy camper. I'm muttering unrepeatable things under my breath through clenched teeth, and, if my megafrown is any indication, I have completely forgotten that—ahem—the Lord loves a cheerful giver (see 2 Cor 9:7).

Now, we moms know perfectly well that life in the mother'hood isn't all unicorns, rainbows, and lollipops. And it's definitely not about perfectly behaved children or having consistent time to accomplish uninterrupted *anything*. Instead, it's often about tracking down missing shoes (again), keeping toddlers from bum-rushing the altar during Mass (again), wiping up frivolous messes (again), and eradicating heinous mystery smells from the van (again). It's about perpetual mountains of laundry, ridiculous to-do lists, and bags under our eyes that are carrying their own unchecked luggage.

I defy anyone to feel supremely "happy" about any of the above circumstances. We give and we give, and then we give some more. And I don't know about you, but I'm not always (ahem) *cheerful* about the giving.

And yet, as Christians, we are told to view *even our hardships* as a reason to rejoice: "Count it all joy, my brethren, when you meet various trials, for you know that the testing of your faith produces steadfastness" (Jas 1:2–3).

At this point, you might be thinking, *I haven't had a good night's sleep in weeks. We don't have enough in our checking account to cover our bills. My kids are driving me crazy. But … God wants me to … count it as …* **joy?**

In a word, *yes*. Now, stick with me here for a minute.

As a young mom, my skin crawled whenever some well-meaning stranger observed my spirited youngsters daring to be youngster-like (usually I was running late when they decided to go full-on *Lord of the Flies* in the grocery store before lunchtime) and felt compelled to offer this gem: "Treasure every! single! minute!" I'd usually grimace and bite the inside of my cheek to keep from pelting the speaker with my exhaustion-fueled litany of grievances. Did she expect me to cherish every blowout diaper, each sleepless night, all ear infections and colicky episodes? How about the countless tantrums and the myriad other energy-sucking maladies of young motherhood? Happy? Happy? Joy? Joy? *Give a tired mom a break.*

You and I both know that it isn't always easy to master our feelings or conform our will to that of our heavenly Father. Our bodies are broken and poured out for our families, often multiple times a day. Yet God wants us to know that, when we rely on *him* as our source of strength (see Neh 8:10) rather than waiting for our circumstances to improve or our feelings to change, we will have abiding joy that the world cannot give. Even when the dinner is burning and the math homework is insanely difficult and the two youngest won't stop touching one other.

So ... what is joy of the Holy Spirit variety, *really?*

Joy isn't a feeling—it's a reality

Now, this isn't some mumbo-jumbo New Age-y concept or a pie-in-the-sky, fortune-cookie phrase. It's Gospel truth about God's kingdom here on earth. Remember: we pray, "Thy kingdom come, thy will be done *on earth as it is in heaven*" (Mt 6:10). Even here on earth, Jesus wants his joy to be in us, and for our joy to be complete (see Jn 15:11).

Yet this joy is not the same as happiness. It took me many, many years to understand this, and I know it's a tough concept. So I repeat: joy and happiness are not one and the same. While happiness comes and goes like the wind, depending on circumstances and feelings—"I just rocked my presentation at work, and the kids aren't biting each other's heads off for a change. I'm so happy!"—joy is an unchangeable reality rooted in our identity as beloved daughters of the Most High God. We belong to him, and one day we hope to be with him in heaven. This is cause for tremendous, incomparable joy! And I can choose to believe and live in that reality ... or not.

Now, there's nothing wrong with happiness—nothing at all! In fact, Jesus talks of happiness when he gives his Sermon on the Mount, specifically the passages about the beatitudes. But happiness on earth is a passing glimpse, a mere hint at the joy that's omnipresent in the kingdom of God.

Ultimately, we can rest in the knowledge that true joy comes from our relationship with a God who loves us beyond our wildest imaginings—that he died and rose so that we can be with him forever in heaven, where everything will be *even more* amazing than unicorns, rainbows, and lollipops. Our ultimate desire isn't for joy—it's for God.

Have you ever wondered how it was possible for so many early Christian martyrs to be unafraid—joyful, even—as they were led to their executions? Because they knew that this earth was not their home. Their real home was with God in heaven, and they were going there soon to be with him forever, so they sang psalms and hymns before the ax struck or the fire burned or the lions pounced.

Not too long ago, our family was afflicted with not one, but two separate flu strains. One kid went down, then the next, and the next. The first kid would begin to recover, only to be knocked back down by the strain that had struck a different kid. And to top it off, a sizable army of invincible ants descended upon our house at the same time. It was a nightmare of near plagues-in-Egypt proportions. Eventually, I was afflicted with a wretched, mutant version of the kids' illnesses and found myself completely down for the count. There was painful coughing, stuffiness, nausea, dizziness, headache, persistent fever, and mucus. *So much mucus!*

Maybe it was the fever, but after the second day of feeling completely useless, I made a decision: I was going to try to squeeze some joy out of this horrid situation even though it was the last thing I felt like doing. I remembered the words of Job 1:21 and made them my own: "The LORD gave me health, and the LORD has taken my health away—blessed be the Name of the LORD." With my scratchy, stuffy, weakened voice, I sang a praise and worship song that brought a smile to my face. Yes, I felt like death warmed over, and, yes, it wasn't my best smile ever, but I *did* smile. Because it all reminded me of the truth: God was still good. He was still in control of the world and my life. He still wanted me to be with him forever in heaven, just maybe not quite yet. And there was nothing the circumstances of my flu-ravaged body could do to change that unchangeable, immeasurably joy-filled truth.

If the joy of the Lord is your strength, don't forget to tell your face

In my many years as a liturgical musician and, more recently, speaking around the country, I've had the tremendous privilege of sharing with God's beloved children, many of whom sit quietly in the pews sporting their very best sour-pickle face. Now, these poor folks look like someone just canceled their birthday. And that's just wrong. None other than Saint Francis of Assisi said, "It is not fitting, when one is in God's service, to have a gloomy face or a chilling look." And we are all, as Pope Francis explains in *The Joy of the Gospel*, in God's service by virtue of our baptism.

Observing these sad faces makes me wonder: if God is who he says he is, and did for us what Scripture tells us he did—namely, loving us so lavishly that he sent his own Son to die a wretched death for the sole purpose of opening the gates of heaven so we can be with him forever (see Jn 3:16)— why aren't we in a constant state of rejoicing? And when did our faces forget to manifest the joy, joy, joy, joy that is, according to the children's song, down in our hearts? Why in the world would anyone, our children included, freely choose to walk with Christ if they don't see glimmers of joy in our lives? Saint Teresa of Calcutta said, "Joy is a net of love by which you can catch souls." Don't we want our children to be included in that net of joy and love, eventually caught up to heaven? How about our neighbor? How about ourselves?

I hope you answered "yes," and I hope you're smiling about it. If not, let's take a minute to consider practical ways to cultivate joy in your life and put that sour-pickle face to rest for good.

Choosing joy is possible

This just in: choosing joy can be tough! Often, the good, beautiful, and joyful things about motherhood get buried under the crushing weight of an avalanche of responsibility and challenges we weren't quite prepared to face.

It's easy to "choose joy" when all is right with the world. But when kids are screaming at the top of their lungs, and I'm on deadline and forget to eat and morph into "Hangry Mommy" and yell at the kids because we're running late for the fourth appointment of the day, it's super tough to just *decide* to be joyful. Real tough. Throw in something major like chronic depression, illness, unemployment, anxiety, special needs, the unexpected passing of a loved one, or any other number of roadblocks, and choosing joy seems downright impossible. For more about this, please see the Roadblocks toward the end of this chapter.

Thanks be to God, all things *are* possible for him (see Mt 19:26). Most times, even in the midst of great adversity, we can choose to rejoice in the Lord always (see Phil 4:4), with the powerful help of the Holy Spirit.

Sometimes choosing joy looks like taking time for a pit stop so we can reset. You know—doing something to regain a godly perspective on life. Take several deep breaths. Say a prayer. Maybe take a walk around the block or jog a mile or two. Chat with a trusted friend. Go to Mass. Or confession. Or adoration. Or all three. Read Saint Paul's Letter to the Philippians, the book that my friend's pastor calls "The Epistle of Joy." Do *something* that nurtures your spirit and reminds you that God loves you even if the sink is (still) full of dishes and the floors (still) need mopping.

Ask yourself: what brings me real joy? You know that jaunty song Fraulein Maria sings in the movie *The Sound of Music* during the thunderstorm, right? What are a few of *your* favorite things? I can think of my list, and I'm sure, given a minute or two, you could come up with your own as well.

What are the good, true, and beautiful things you enjoy about being a mom? Do you like going places and experiencing things with your kids? Do more of that! How about singing songs with them or having impromptu dance parties in the kitchen? Put that on the agenda for today if you can. Maybe you like cooking with them, or crafting, or hanging out at the park, or reading aloud, or visiting friends. Do more of the things that fill you with joy and fewer of the things that steal it away. At the very least, once your precious ones succumb to slumber, you can find some joy in knowing that y'all made it to nap/rest/bed and … bonus … you're still alive.

When all else fails, we can choose to act *as if*. We can smile as if we remember how much God loves us and how blessed we really are, even when we aren't feeling it. My mom used to call it "fake it till you make it." And while I can't point to the Scripture verse where Jesus says, "Amen, amen I say to you: pretend you are joyful and joy will be yours," what if making an act of the will to smile, even when we don't feel like it, is an outward sign of an inward grace? What if, with that choice, we invite the Holy Spirit to work in our hearts, watering the seed we've planted and allowing the fruit of joy to grow?

● ● ●

Roadblocks to cultivating joy

Sometimes we can block our own ability to live in the reality of God's joy. Here are some common culprits:

Negativity: Nobody likes a nattering nabob of negativism. Constantly whining and complaining can render joy (ours and others') dead on arrival. The Letter of James, which talks a lot about the power of our speech, is quite explicit: "Do not grumble" (5:9). Instead, we can strive to follow Saint Paul's advice to the Philippians: "Finally, brethren, whatever is true, whatever is honorable, whatever is just, whatever is pure, whatever is lovely, whatever is gracious, if there is any excellence, if there is anything worthy of praise, think about these things" (4:8). You've heard the saying, "Garbage in, garbage out," right? If we find ourselves fighting off Eeyore-like gloom, it might be time to edit what we're allowing into our lives. Practically speaking, this could mean unfollowing, unsubscribing, and outright banning any media that threatens to drive us off the road toward joy.

Poor self-talk: Speaking of the power of speech, when was the last time you said something positive to yourself about your vocation as a mom? Maybe you're amazing at encouraging others, but you fall short when you need encouragement yourself. Poor self-talk—*I'm a terrible mom, I can't do this, I'm going to mess my kids up,* etc., etc.—flies in the face of your identity as beloved daughter of the Most High God, unconditionally and madly loved by your heavenly Father and fully capable of handling the tasks he sets before you. And I know this for sure: God doesn't make junk. This includes YOU. If you need some roadside assistance on this journey to joy, get your hands on *I AM,* by Chris Stefanick, and see how revamping the messages you tell yourself *about* yourself can change your life.

Coveting: There's nothing like reallllly wanting another mom's Pinterest-worthy kitchen or birthday party or hairdo or wardrobe or vacation or career or *whatever* to put the brakes on joy. When we avoid dangerous detours like envy, bitterness, and resentment, we're much more likely to arrive in a place of authentic joy.

Ingratitude: Being ungrateful for the many blessings God has given us is like crumpling up the master map that leads us to joy and throwing it right out the window. Try spending more time thanking and praising God to get back on track. More about this in a later chapter.

People pleasing and perfectionism: When we constantly

worry about what other people want, need, think, or will approve, we have less fuel to seek after what God wants to give us in our vocation. Saint Paul addresses this very thing in Galatians 1:10: "Am I now seeking the favor of men, or of God? Or am I trying to please men? If I were still pleasing men, I should not be a servant of Christ." Let's seek to please God alone, walking in his will for us, and watch the joy expound!

Attachments: It's much more difficult to enter into the joy of the Lord when we cling to things of this world, pet sins, or anything that is not of God's kingdom. Are you having an especially rough time detaching from bad habits or attitudes? Now might be a good time to drive on over to the nearest parish for confession. Nothing brings joy to the soul quite like complete reconciliation and time spent with the Lord. Check out www.masstimes.org to find Mass, confession, or adoration at a parish near you.

Living in the past and/or worrying about the future: We may find that things that once brought us joy simply don't anymore, or that accomplishing everyday tasks is grueling or even downright impossible. Trust me—I've been there. It could be that you're suffering from depression, anxiety, or another challenge to your mental health. In such cases, you genuinely can't just "choose" to be joyful. I want you to know: there's absolutely no shame in reaching out for help or admitting you're hurting. Suffering with mental-health challenges doesn't mean you're a bad person. It doesn't mean you aren't trying hard enough to be better. It doesn't mean that you aren't praying hard enough to be healed, or that you just aren't holy enough. It also doesn't mean that God is punishing you or no longer loves you. It doesn't mean you're a bad person, a bad wife, or a bad mother. Sometimes we just need extra help and support to find our way. Just as you'd seek assistance if you had a physical ailment, it is important to seek mental-health care and let a professional help bring your body and mind back into balance. I believe it brings

God great joy when we choose to take care of his children (and that includes ourselves).

In addition, please don't ever hesitate to check in and reach out to other moms with a text, a call, or a visit. Often, people won't reach out to anyone when they're hurting, because that's a common side effect of their illness. Let them know they are loved, that you care, that you want to help. Accompany them as best you can, and don't be afraid to seek out professionals for assistance.

Saint Dymphna, patroness of mental-health sufferers, pray for us.

● ● ●

Yield to the power of the Holy Spirit

(prayer)

Dearest Jesus,
Sometimes I feel like joy has been sucked out of my life like juice from an orange. I'm giving to my family, but I'm not always cheerful about it. Lord, I want to be a more joyful mom. I know that trials will come and go, but I believe that your love for me and my family remains. I know that I won't always experience feelings of happiness, but I know that joy is possible, even in the most difficult moments, when I keep my eyes firmly fixed on you and your promises. I know that, even in the hardest times, Jesus, you want my joy to be complete.

Come, Holy Spirit—fill me with your joy. Amen.

● ● ●

GPS: God Positioning System

(scripture)

"You show me the path of life;

in your presence there is fulness of joy,
in your right hand are pleasures for evermore."
— Psalms 16:11

"Rejoice in the Lord always; again, I will say, Rejoice."
— Philippians 4:4

"The joy of the Lord is your strength." — Nehemiah 8:10

"Weeping may last for the night,
but joy comes with the morning." — Psalms 30:5

● ● ●

Roadside Assistance

(wisdom from the saints and others)

"The joy promised by the beatitudes is the very joy of Jesus himself: a joy sought and found in obedience to the Father, and in the gift of self to others." — Pope Saint John Paul II

"If we wish to serve God and love our neighbor well, we must manifest our joy in the service we render to him and them. Let us open wide our hearts. It is joy which invites us. Press forward and fear nothing." — Saint Katharine Drexel

● ● ●

Pit Stop

(other resources)

- Read *I AM* by Chris Stefanick for daily Scripture-based reflections affirming our identity in Christ Jesus. This book has brought much joy to my life! If your family likes read-aloud stories, my friend recommends *Saint Philip of the Joyous Heart* by Francis Xavier Connolly. It's a highly rated tale about Saint Philip Neri, someone who radiated the joy and love of the Lord.

- Watch *The Sound of Music* or another uplifting, feel-good movie, either by yourself or (even better!) with your kids. Make popcorn, snuggle on the couch, and talk about some of your favorite things.

- Listen to or sing some praise and worship music—there are many free online resources and playlists available. Bonus points if you find an upbeat mix and begin an impromptu dance party with your kids in the living room!

- The next time you're praying, consider meditating on the Joyful Mysteries of the Rosary. Use your imagination to visualize yourself observing the joy of Mary at the Annunciation; Mary and Elizabeth at the Visitation; Mary, Joseph, the shepherds and the host of angels at the Nativity; Mary, Joseph, Simeon, and Anna at the Presentation; and Mary and Joseph at the Finding of the Child Jesus in the Temple.

- Check out Pope Francis' apostolic exhortation *The Joy of the Gospel*. Maybe a friend or two would like to get together and talk about it over a cup of tea or a glass of wine. Discuss how you could apply some of what you read to encourage a more joy-filled life in Christ.

● ● ●

Your Ideas

_____

_____

_____

_____

_____

_____

_____

_____

_____

• • •

Discuss Amongst Yourselves

(questions)

1. Consider that which is good, true, and beautiful about your life as a mom. List the things that bring you supreme joy.

2. Which roadblocks throw you off the road toward joy most often? What can you do about it?

3. What is one thing you can do this week to cultivate more joy in your vocation? ("Drink more coffee" doesn't count. Ha, ha.)

CAUTION: MERGE AHEAD

((humility))

"One thing they never tell you about child raising is that for the rest of your life, at the drop of a hat, you are expected to know your child's name and how old he or she is."

— Erma Bombeck

• • •

I could never be holy … could I?

Now, before we get too terribly far down the road, let's talk about humility. While not a fruit of the Holy Spirit, humility is a virtue often associated with the cardinal virtue of temperance. Sounds exciting, huh?

Before you skip to the next chapter, thinking that humility is for *other* people (like that mom who thinks she's all that and a plate of homemade gluten-free cookies for the whole class), take it from someone who used to avoid praying for humility like it was rabies, influenza, and a trigonometry test all rolled into one. Humility often gets a bad rap, especially in today's WIIFM (what's in it for me) culture. All the more reason, then, to put away false definitions and misunderstandings and learn about what humility actually is and why we so desperately need it.

In my case, I grew up Christian and knew that pride equals *bad* and humility equals *good*. I also knew that pretty much all the saints emphasized humility as an important key to spiritual growth. But what did being humble actually look like? Since I am *not* a saint, I thought being humble meant I had to stop being, well, *me*. I'm frequently loud, and I stink at being still. In school, I was often reprimanded for talking. My mom called it verbal diarrhea. That hurt my feelings. Except now, when I hear my kids doing it, I know exactly what she was talking about. And she was right. Sorry, Mom.

Anyway, I was voted "Most likely to be the next Weird Al Yankovic" in eighth grade, a title I actually campaigned to win. I sang solos in choir, was drum major in band, and loved performing in school musicals and plays. I was president of Spanish Club and was the districtwide storytelling contest champ not once but twice. I wasn't exactly a shrinking violet. Surely, I was too loud and obnoxious to ever be *holy*!

Also problematic, in my mind, were my many faults. I was stubborn, forgetful, easily distracted, a perfectionist and people pleaser, and tended to put off things until the last minute. I'd begin projects with the best intentions, yet struggle to follow through. And that was just the beginning of my confessional list.

For a very long time, I thought someone with my personality and sinful hang-ups didn't have a chance in you-know-where to gain heaven. It wasn't that I didn't believe that Jesus died for my sins; I did believe that—wholeheartedly—but somehow, I just didn't think I would be allowed in the pearly gates unless I picked the lock. At which point I would be kicked out for trying to cheat the system, so what was the point in trying?

As I gazed upon statues of the beautiful, serene, sinless Virgin Mary and read stories about pure, obedient, perfectly behaved saints, I figured I just didn't have what it took. I wasn't quiet enough, gentle enough, patient enough, demure enough, obedient enough, or holy enough. I determined the best I could hope for was to scrape into purgatory by the skin of my teeth. Then I discovered Mother Angelica of EWTN fame, and I started to believe it might be possible for a boisterous, stubborn, somewhat quirky Italian American who cackled at her own jokes to be a devoted follower of Christ. On the counsel of a wise priest during confession, I started looking for holy women who weren't, by any means, perfect. They just knew who they were and they knew who God was, and they allowed the Holy Spirit to mold and change them.

Living in the school of humility

It turns out I suffered from a severe case of what some call "upside-down" pride. It was sort of like life was a scene from one of Oprah's big giveaway shows. I was watching God tell the excited crowd, "You get holiness! And you get forgiveness! And you get grace! And you! And you!" But none of that was meant for me. Somehow, I was the only one not good enough to receive God's blessings. Maybe I'd get a toaster oven as a consolation prize, but that was about it. This entire concept was, of course, ridiculous and, ironically, extremely prideful. I mean, who did I think I was, genuinely believing that everybody else in the universe was worthy of receiving the mercy, love, and grace of God, yet somehow, I wasn't?

This revelation forced me to admit: I didn't fully trust that God was who he said he was. I spent so much time and energy focused on my shortcomings and sinfulness that I forgot he is the Creator of the universe—the Alpha and the Omega, the beginning and the end. The Savior and lover of my soul. My rock. My salvation. My fortress. My deliverer. He can forgive and heal whomever he wants, even a wretched sinner like me. I was not exempt from his kingship. I was not too far gone for his mercy. I just had to get over myself—and quick.

He must increase, I must decrease

You've heard of the Litany of Humility, right? If you haven't, look it up. It talks about scary things like detaching from our own desires, wanting God to prefer others to us, asking for other people to be admired and respected and acknowledged instead of us, and many other truly horrible things. I avoided this prayer like none other. I wouldn't go near it with a fifty-foot pole. I mean, I already had a gaggle of children who humiliated me on a regular basis. And besides, I am who I am. And being me means I can embarrass myself at least ten times a day without even trying. I mean, not too long ago, I went to an important meeting only to realize afterward that my fly was down the whole time. It made me think that perhaps I should only wear skirts. But knowing me, I'd find a way to humiliate myself with an epic wardrobe malfunction regardless of my attire. At any rate, I already felt inadequate in my vocation, and quite lonely. Why would I want to pray for these Truly Horrible Things? So I could feel even *worse* about myself?? I was pretty sure I didn't need any more opportunities for humiliation, thanks.

And then one day at a mom's group, my friend whipped out prayer books for everybody and pointed us to a page where we'd begin our prayer time. And there was the dreaded Litany of Humility, staring me in the face.

Talk about being blindsided.

The group wasn't big enough for me to fade into the background as I would have liked. I was going to have to swallow my—*ooh!* What was my hesitation? Pride? Fear?—and pray this (in my opinion) stupid, scary, soul-squashing prayer.

Except as we began, the prayer didn't seem so stupid anymore. Awkward, yes. Difficult, absolutely. But not stupid. I sensed the words of this long-avoided litany gently yet insistently chipping away at some hard places within my heart. As tears filled my eyes and spilled out onto my cheeks, I began to realize that what God wanted to cultivate within my soul was not a spirit of shame, guilt, or self-loathing, but a spirit of deeper acceptance and peace—acceptance both of him as my merciful heavenly Father and of myself as his precious, little child. And in that knowledge, he wanted me to rest in his abiding love.

Praying the Litany of Humility wasn't about being humiliated in the "dangit, I messed up again" sense of the word. It was about asking the Holy Spirit to give me grace to remember my identity as a beloved daughter of the Most High God. It was about understanding that without God, I can do *nothing* (see Jn 15:5), but I *can* do all things through Christ (see Phil 4:13). And that I could drive that understanding of who God is and who I am to the bank every single time and never be shortchanged.

Humiliations galore

Being a parent is a bizarre and tremendous thing. All of a sudden, you're expected to be completely responsible for someone you've just met, who has all manner of needs that you've (at least in my case) never supplied before. To top it off, your darling begins to exhibit various personality traits and proclivities that surely don't come from your sweet side of the gene pool.

But, as I mentioned earlier, necessity is a mother. I am a mother, because my children were conceived. And I had to figure out how to be a mother; because, presto change-o, I was one.

It's truly baffling how such utterly tiny and helpless beings can somehow reduce grown-ups to puddles incapable of rational thought, but they can. And do. At least, they do in my family. Regularly.

I can think of very few things more humbling than taking a rowdy crew of overtired youngsters to Mass. Or a restaurant. Or a grocery store. Or anywhere in public, frankly, and many private locations as well.

Just the other day, we pulled into our perfectly private garage, and one of my favorite songs was playing on the Christian radio station. I parked the van and decided to finish singing along with the song before going into the house.

Just for fun, I recorded a snippet to post on social media, thinking the song might lift someone else's spirits, too. There I was, dancing and singing along, when I heard my preschooler's voice: "Mom! You're shaaaaking the whoooole caaaaar!"

Kids just have a way of stripping you down and helping you keep it real. Like, *really* real. Know what I mean?

Comedian Jim Gaffigan said: "You know what it's like having a fourth kid? Imagine you're drowning, then someone hands you a baby." Welcoming child after child after child meant that I finally had to admit the truth: I didn't have it all together. I didn't really know what I was doing or even where I was going at all times. Most days, I was flying by the seat of my too-tight pants, hoping to make it through the day without mortally wounding themselves, a sibling, or their primary caregiver (me). For a recovering perfectionistic people-pleaser, admitting that I was swimming beyond my depths was a difficult pill to swallow. I liked being in control of my environment, my time, and my to-do list. Yet my precious children didn't really seem to care too much about deadlines, appointments, and wearing shoes that match.

Now, I don't want to imply that, at any point, I would ever admit defeat at the sticky hands of the small army my husband and I have created. No way; I'm too stubborn for that. But, thanks be to God, I have finally come to realize that I cannot do it on my own; and, perhaps more importantly, I don't have to.

There's a platitude that goes, "God never gives us more than we can handle." Nice, right? Here's another one: "If he leads us to it, he'll lead us through it," and all that. Well, I would agree that God allows things to happen and comes to our aid because he's a good Father. But I would also say that we are often insecure and prideful and pile things on ourselves that God never intended for us to take on, including expectations of ourselves as wives and mothers … as human beings in general.

That's where, surprisingly enough, humility comes in. My *fiat*—my "yes" to God—won't look like yours, and *your fiat* won't look like anyone else's, either. We have to make our "yes" our own; otherwise, it's incomplete at best and a forgery at worst. For me, learning to say "yes" to God's call to mother my children looks an awful lot like becoming who God wants me to be: more humble. More loving. More patient, gentle, and kind.

Author Bob Goff writes, "We're all rough drafts of the people we're becoming." Some of us are rougher drafts than others. But the good news is that God's still working on steering us in the right direction, as long as we allow him.

Real humility lets me live the truth that I don't have to be anyone but Heather. And you don't have to be anyone but you. Sure, there will always be things that need to be refined, but God sent us our spouses, children, friends, ministers, coworkers, and even strangers on the street to help see to our spiritual growth, if we submit to the process. And just because we won't be perfect this side of heaven doesn't mean God is going to drop us like a bad habit. He loved us enough to die for us while we were still sinners, after all (see Rom 5:8). And he is not ever, ever going to abandon us or forsake us, not even at the first whiff of a dirty diaper or the hint of another epic meltdown, even if it's ours. He is in it with us for the long haul.

As this realization has settled in, I've found that I no longer obsess about my faults and failings. I can accept my talents and gifts. And as I've done that, something incredible has happened: I don't think about myself so much. I still have a long way to go, but I am starting to believe that whatever I'm meant to accomplish has more to do with who God is and much less to do with my human frailties. I've stopped focusing so much on what I can't do and more on who God *is*.

Frankly, I don't care so much anymore if my laugh is kind of loud, or if I shake the van because I'm praising God. I care more about living in the truth of God's love and sharing that love with my family and neighbors. At the end of the day, the most humbling thing in my entire life is that God blessed me with the five uniquely challenging, beautifully precious souls who call me Mama. What an amazing grace.

Of course, I still struggle with pride, and some days the words of the Litany of Humility are especially hard to pray. One thing I've found helpful is to listen and sing along with a beautiful song called "I Shall Not Want" by Audrey Assad, which incorporates lines from the prayer. And then I listen to "Good to Me," Audrey's next track, about how loving and patient God is with me. Since Saint Augustine said that "he who sings prays twice," I figure I'm covering my bases more or less, right? Obviously, God isn't finished with me yet.

P.S. Making peace with Saint Thérèse of Lisieux

Please don't revoke my Catholic card when I admit that my first impression of Saint Thérèse was … "meh." While friends and acquaintances were going on and on and on about this saint and her "Little Way" and how it was increasing their faith, I wasn't particularly impressed. She struck me as sheltered, somewhat spoiled, and far too flowery in her writing. And then there was all this "sacrificing" business. Thérèse willingly offered to take on the dirtiest, most difficult jobs in Carmel. I was a modern, American, boisterous, extroverted mother of five. My unspoken motto was, "Go big or go home." I only did the dirtiest and most difficult things if I absolutely had to. What in the world could I possibly have in common with a nineteenth-century cloistered nun from France?

I decided to focus on and emulate women I could actually relate to, like the courageous Joan of Arc and gregarious, outspoken Mother Angelica. Even tiny Mother Teresa seemed like she could be a bit of a stinker, you know? She always had that twinkle in her eye, like she was up to something. I could dig that. But sweet, innocent Thérèse? I decided that, no offense to her or her fan club, my feelings wouldn't be hurt if she chose to be friends with other people instead of me.

Then I learned that Thérèse was not only a Doctor of the Church, but patroness of missionaries. I didn't get it. But as a faithful daughter of Rome and enthusiastic ambassador for the New Evangelization, I felt I had a responsibility to figure out why she was so esteemed by Holy Mother Church. What was it about this simple girl that struck such a chord with so many of the faithful?

The more I researched, the more I realized just how applicable Thérèse's Little Way of small sacrifices was for busy moms like me. I was already on board with offering things up, at least in theory. But there was something about how Father Michael Gaitley unpacked Thérèse's philosophy in his book *33 Days to Merciful Love* that really resonated with me. The Divine Mercy devotion had me at "hello," yet Father Gaitley's explanations about Thérèse helped me see her with fresh eyes. This little Carmelite nun was growing on me.

After finishing Father Gaitley's book, I decided to intentionally "offer up" every time I picked up toys, scrubbed counters, folded laundry, cooked dinner, consoled a child, or any of the countless, sometimes ridiculous things required of a mom on any given day. I would try to, as Saint Teresa of Calcutta said (inspired, no doubt, by Thérèse), "Do small things with great love." Even if I never set foot out of my house (my cloister—ha!), I could still offer up my small sacrifices for Jesus, just like Thérèse.

Many days, I don't get much done in the eyes of the world. Children are clothed (usually) and fed (often) and bathed (occasionally). But I can keep up with one small thing at a time. I can feed the hungry, give sippy cups to the thirsty, clothe the naked, visit the imprisoned (toddlers in cribs come to mind), and offer it all up as a loving sacrifice to the Lord. When done with surrender and cheerfulness, these little actions make me a missionary of love and mercy right within the walls of my own home.

In hindsight, I think I knew, deep down, that I was more like young Thérèse than I wanted to admit. But it freaked me out, so I ran in the other direction. Like Thérèse, I lived a pretty sheltered life as a kid, and I was also prone to tantrums and theatrics. I, too, had an early encounter with the Blessed Mother (that's for another book, I suppose), and I suffered with abandonment issues due to being adopted. She and I were both writers, after a fashion. And we both wanted to spread the Good News of Jesus. At a certain point, I could no longer deny that we were truly sisters in Christ in more ways than I previously understood.

But the clincher on our friendship, I think, was when I realized this little nugget: I'd been clinging to a small card I received when I was a child that said my name means, "Joyful Spirit." But the name "Heather" also means ... wait for it ... *little flower.*

I think Saint Thérèse and Jesus had a really good, long laugh when I figured out that one. She taught me that I can learn many things from all sorts of holy people, even those with whom I thought I had zilch in common. And her Little Way, when I choose to employ it, helps me stay faithful in the small things. It's interesting what happens when you allow the Holy Spirit to hijack your heart, isn't it?

● ● ●

Roadblock to humility

Pride: You knew this one was coming, right? Pride is called the mother of all sins because nearly every other sin can trace its roots back to our good friend, pride. Except pride ain't no friend—it's an unrepentant killer. When one is prideful, she thinks she is in charge, in control. In essence, taken to the nth degree, a prideful person thinks she is, at least in one way or another, above and beyond God. Everyone must be on the lookout for various forms of pride. Praying to the Holy Spirit for the grace to detach from ourselves so we may develop the right sense of who we are (children of God) and who he is (Almighty God) is key.

• • •

Yield to the power of the Holy Spirit
(prayer)

Dear Lord,
Thank you for the gift of my life and my vocation. Please reveal the truth to me as I go about my ministry as wife and mother. When I forget who I am, please remind me. When I forget who you are, please show me. Help me to focus less on my faults and failings and more on your power and might. I believe you love me just as I am and are shaping me into who I am meant to be. Help me humble myself to become love for my family, made after your image and likeness. Thank you for being such a good and faithful Father to me.

Come, Holy Spirit—make me truly humble. Amen.

• • •

GPS: God Positioning System
(scripture)

"He must increase, but I must decrease." — John 3:30

"It is no longer I who live, but Christ who lives in me." — Galatians 2:20

"Whoever exalts himself will be humbled, and whoever humbles himself will be exalted." — Matthew 23:12

"For apart from me you can do nothing." — John 15:5

"Good and upright is the LORD;
therefore he instructs sinners in the way.
He leads the humble in what is right,
and teaches the humble his way." — Psalms 25:8–9

"God said to Moses, 'I AM WHO I AM.'" — Exodus 3:14

"Clothe yourselves, all of you, with humility toward one another, for 'God opposes the proud, but gives grace to the humble.' Humble yourselves therefore under the mighty hand of God, that in due time he may exalt you. Cast all your anxieties on him, for he cares about you." — 1 Peter 5:5–7

"I am the Alpha and the Omega, the first and the last, the beginning and the end." — Revelation 22:13

• • •

Roadside Assistance

(wisdom from the saints and others)

"If you are humble nothing will touch you, neither praise nor disgrace, because you know what you are."
— Saint Teresa of Calcutta

"If you should ask me what are the ways of God, I would tell you that the first is humility, the second is humility, and the third is humility. Not that there are no other precepts to give, but if humility does not precede all that we do, our efforts are meaningless." — Saint Augustine

"To rely on our talents is a cause of great loss. When someone places confidence in his own prudence, knowledge, and intelligence, God, to make him know and see his insufficiency, withdraws from him his help and leaves him to work by himself. This is often why our undertakings miserably fail." — Saint Vincent de Paul

"It is by humility that the Lord allows himself to be conquered, so that he will do all we ask of him."
— Saint Teresa of Ávila

"We are not the sum of our weaknesses and failures, we are the sum of the Father's love for us and our real capacity to become the image of his Son." — Pope Saint John Paul II

"What a man is before God, that he is, and nothing more."
— Saint Francis of Assisi

"Do not desire to be what you are; desire to be very well what you are." — Saint Francis de Sales

"These are the few ways we can practice humility:
To speak as little as possible of one's self.
To mind one's own business.
Not to want to manage other people's affairs.
To avoid curiosity.
To accept contradictions and correction cheerfully.
To pass over the mistakes of others.
To accept insults and injuries.
To accept being slighted, forgotten, and disliked.
To be kind and gentle even under provocation.
Never to stand on one's dignity.
To choose always the hardest."
— Saint Teresa of Calcutta

● ● ●

Pit Stop

(other resources)

- Listen to the song "I Shall Not Want" by Audrey Assad from her *Fortunate Fall* album. Bonus: Listen to the next track, "Good to Me."

- One of my favorite songs is "Lord, I Need You" by Matt Maher. Meditate on the words and make it a prayer from your heart.

- Read *33 Days to Merciful Love* by Father Michael Gaitley, MIC, to learn more about my friend (hopefully she doesn't mind me calling her that) Saint Thérèse and the true nature of our loving and merciful God.

- Consider Saint Teresa of Calcutta's tips for practicing humility from her book *The Joy in Loving: A Guide to Daily Living*.

• • •

Your Ideas

_____

_____

_____

• • •

Discuss Amongst Yourselves
(questions)

1. Author C. S. Lewis said that a truly humble person "will not be thinking about humility: he will not be thinking about himself at all." How might we apply this concept in our lives as wives and mothers without sacrificing our physical, spiritual, or mental health?

2. Where do you find yourself struggling to exercise humility? Are there areas where you are too self-focused, critical, worried, or anxious? How might you address those speed bumps this week?

3. How is God revealing to you the truth of who he is and who you are through your vocation?

SLOW DOWN

((peace))

"I never know what to say when people ask me what my hobbies are. I mean, I'm a mom. I enjoy trips to the bathroom alone, and silence."

— *Unknown*

• • •

L et's just get this out of the way: I'm a talker. I know— you're shocked, right? I can tell.

Anyway, if you want to jam about life until well past last call, I'm your girl. And while I will politely hang with you for a few minutes if you'd rather chitchat, I'd much rather spend time digging in to the meat and potatoes of life with you. I like to go *deep*.

During my early years of motherhood, however, the only deep things on my radar were the piles of diapers, laundry, and dishes. And there was noise. Lots, and lots, and lots, and lots of noise. Did I mention it was noisy? Our two little girls, twenty-one months apart, had well-formed lungs and vocal chords that they liked to exercise. Loudly. And often.

Sadly, "conduct fulfilling conversations with attentive, well-reasoned adults" didn't make the cut for my job description as Chief Minister of Interruptions for the Renshaw household.

Most days, going somewhere—anywhere—in search of connection with other adults felt like an insurmountable undertaking. Attending the parish moms' group, the toddler playdate, or the meetup at the park meant the little people and I had to be presentable, likable, and relatable. All at the same time. It seemed like an awful lot of "ables" for someone who often felt like she was drowning in a sea of inability. So we often stayed home, save for the occasional white-knuckle trip to the grocery store or the doctor's office. And there was great wailing and gnashing of teeth.

I don't remember what prompted me to finally seek spiritual direction with Sister Therese at a local retreat house several years ago, but on some level, I knew something had to change. I was depleted, lonely, and in a major funk. After we met for six fruitful weeks, Sister recommended I attend an on-site weekend women's retreat as a "capstone" of sorts for our one-on-one sessions. I liked the idea of diving deeper into the Faith, but I was even more excited to engage with like-minded Catholic women.

With family life and a part-time job draining every last drop of my energy and brain power, the prospect of sustained interaction with adults and some time to myself was more appealing than a fat stack of cash. To my surprise and delight, it didn't take much to convince my husband that I should go. One phone call and I was all set to attend my very first retreat alone.

The following Friday, after David arrived home from work, I quickly kissed him and the girls goodbye and hopped in "the little car" with enthusiasm outweighing my overnight bag. This, I told myself, was going to be a treat—sort of like a girls' night out, only a *whole day and a half*. And *Catholic*.

So the odds of someone getting arrested were, in my mind, somewhat diminished.

Upon arrival at the retreat house, I was welcomed with a warm embrace by one of the sisters, assigned a room, and handed a schedule. There was about forty-five minutes before dinner, so I decided to stroll the grounds. During my walkabout, I noticed other women taking advantage of the late September sunshine and serene, park-like setting. While I didn't recognize any of the ladies offhand, I smiled to myself, anticipating the conversations we'd have about *whatever*. It honestly didn't matter *what* we discussed, so long as it wasn't *Sesame Street*, My Little Pony, or potty training.

At dinner, I found myself eating a warm meal that I didn't have to cook myself, surrounded by seven wonderful women, each lovelier and more fascinating than the last. We were laughing and digging in to delicious apple crisp a la mode for dessert when Sister Anne Marie rang a bell to attract our attention. "Ladies," she said with a smile, "we hope you enjoyed your meal."

Everyone nodded and murmured appreciation through bites of warm apple crisp. She continued, "We also hope you enjoyed your conversation, because once we clear the dishes, we will enter into The Silence."

Huh?

Did she say ... *silence?* With ... no talking? What did that mean? We couldn't speak? That night? Or *the whole weekend?*

One of the women at my table noticed my jaw dragging on the tablecloth beneath me, dessert fork suspended in space between my mouth and my plate. "Have you ever been to a silent retreat, Heather?" she asked. I was still trying to comprehend what I thought Sister said. *Silent.* A women's retreat with *no talking?* Wasn't that, like, an oxymoron or something?

I placed my fork on the plate, gooey bite still intact, and assured my dinner companion that, no, I had *not* been on a silent retreat ever before in my life; that, in fact, this was my very first retreat alone in eons. She nodded and smiled, saying, "Oh, you're going to love it. Especially since you have little ones. The silence is so peaceful."

Except I didn't *want* to be quiet. I wanted to talk! I wanted to meet other women and have amazing conversations into the wee hours of the morning and maybe even bond with a few of them and make friends! There had to be an explanation. I quickly deduced that either this was one of the circles of hell, or someone would be popping out with a camera to tell me I was being pranked. *Gotcha!* they'd say, and we'd all have a good laugh and go about having our grown-up conversations regarding interesting things.

How could I have signed up for the only silent women's event on the retreat house schedule without realizing it? The word "silent" was definitely *not* on the flier I showed my husband, because had it been, we would both have died laughing at the absurdity of me, chatty Cathy herself, on a silent retreat. Interestingly, my dear spiritual director hadn't mentioned silence, either.

I wiped my mouth with my cloth napkin, smiled a fake smile at no one in particular, and excused myself from the table. There was only one thing to do: I had to find Sister Therese.

The lights in the corridors were already dimmed for the evening, but I easily found my way to the familiar room with Sister's name on the door.

I'd barely raised my right hand to knock when the door swung open, and there was Sister Therese, smiling up at me. "Ah, Heather!" she said as she leaned in for a hug. "You made it!" "Yes, yes, Sister, thank you," I responded, "I made it." And then I had to take a bit of a deep breath to calm down, because I was pretty sure it was a major sin to yell at a nun. "Um, Sister," I began carefully. "You never told me this was a SILENT retreat." Sister Therese cocked her head slightly to the left, then back to center again, never breaking eye contact with me. "Si-lent," I repeated, in case she missed it. "As in, *no talking.*"

"Hmmm," she responded with a slight shake of her head. "I didn't? I thought I did." I couldn't tell whether the glimmer in her eye was because of how the light from the hall reflected on her face, or because she'd plotted to bamboozle me all along.

"No, Sister," I protested. "You definitely didn't tell me. I would never have come if I knew it was a silent retreat!"

"Ah, I see," she said, nodding. "Well, Heather, your husband is taking care of the girls, yes? And you are already here. Is your room to your liking?" she paused, awaiting my response.

"Yes, Sister," I replied, trying to appear more grateful than I felt.

"So, since you are already here, why don't you try it out? If it gets too hard, Heather, you can always come find me, and I will talk to you." She smiled to let me know our conversation was done.

Looking down at this small yet earnest Filipino woman who looked like a close relative of my dearly departed grandmother, I knew arguing would get me nowhere.

"Okay, Sister Therese," I said, resigned to my fate. "I will try."

"Good, Heather," Sister Therese said with an even bigger smile. "Don't worry—I will ask my Honey to help you," she said, referring to Jesus, her groom, as she often did. "You should get some sleep, Heather. You look tired."

"Yes, Sister. Thank you, Sister." I smiled weakly and walked toward my room on the other side of the building. Other retreatants smiled at me and nodded as we passed one another in the corridor, gestures I halfheartedly imitated. The dreaded Silence had begun.

I'm not sure whether you've ever remained silent for an entire weekend; perhaps that sounds like heaven on earth to you! For me, though, at the time, it was unsettling and quite terrifying. Suddenly, I was thrust into a scenario without television, phone, friends, family, and snacks. All of my usual distractions were gone. What I did have was a tsunami of swirling thoughts and emotions and anxieties threatening to eat me alive. I didn't sleep very well.

The next morning, we gathered in the chapel for Morning Prayer, a practice with which I was unaccustomed. Our group recited the prescribed prayers and listened to Scripture passages for about twenty minutes, remaining silent as we walked from the chapel to the dining room.

Breakfast was served, napkins acquired, juice and coffee poured, utensils clinked. And all in utter silence. It was … creepy. And wondrous. And so completely foreign. Whereas I was used to the incessant maelstrom of tiny voices calling, jabbering, screaming, crying, laughing, whooping, and whining, mashed up with cartoons, kid songs, and related earworms … this absence of sound was bizarre and disconcerting.

It took nearly the whole of Saturday—three presentations from the retreat master priest, three meals, solitary time walking on the grounds, lying on my bed in my little cell staring up at the ceiling, going to confession for the first time in months, praying the Stations of the Cross and the Rosary, attending daily Mass, and spending time in adoration—for my internal state to begin to match my outside environment. The troop of hyperactive monkeys swinging from branch to branch to branch in my brain slowed, then stopped, then disappeared completely, replaced with … what? *What was this sensation?*

It was calm. It was a lack of incessant, extraneous sound and mess in my brain for the first time in who knows how long. It was, dare I say, *peace.* And then the most marvelous thing happened—I could hear nudges of the Holy Spirit in ways I'd never experienced before. Instead of me dumping my grocery list of prayers at his feet like I usually did, I was quiet. And listening. And hearing something in return.

It turns out God wasn't in the mighty wind of the world rushing past me, nor was he in the earthquake of the latest kid crisis. He wasn't in the fire of my best-laid plans burning down around me, either. He was in the quiet whisper that I couldn't hear through the noise lodged within my heart.

What Sister Therese knew that I didn't know was that, while connecting with other women might have been fun, connecting with Jesus was life-changing.

Searching for and maintaining peace

I believe God knew the exact number of children and life circumstances it would take for me to finally surrender and run *toward* the calm and quiet of the adoration chapel, the empty sanctuary, or the secluded park rather than away from them. He knew that, given the chaos and messiness of family life, I'd finally learn to embrace silence rather than cram my days with even more noise.

Anyone who knows us knows that my husband and I can be loud people. So it really shouldn't be a huge surprise, given our gene pool, that the Renshaw children can be loud, loud, loud, loud, and louder. At least they come by it honestly. Our home is not quiet. We do not do "inside voices" well. And, if your "family-mobile" is anything like mine, it just might be the noisiest place on planet earth. There have been countless times when I have threatened to kick everyone out of the van, because I can't take the noise anymore. I keep praying that someone will invent a soundproof privacy window that I can install between me and my rambunctious passengers—sort of like they have for limousines—in my minivan. But if I'm honest, there are times when my children are quietly turning pages of the hymnal during Mass and it sounds to me like they're jackhammering the sidewalk. As I discovered on my silent retreat, the absence of external noise doesn't guarantee inner calm.

Maintaining the peace I'd cultivated at the retreat house once I returned home was … challenging. Just because Mommy tasted the sweet, sacred cup of silence didn't mean that my people magically became saintly practitioners of calm. Silence in a busy household is often elusive. But what I've found is I can seek out the quiet place in my heart whenever I want, whenever I remember I can, because I know it's there;

God is there. Waking up before the children to pray the Morning Offering and reading Scripture helps establish calm before busyness takes hold. Stealing a few minutes of quiet in my self-declared cone of silence (aka our bedroom) while my husband corrals the crew after dinner helps, too. I've found there are countless opportunities sprinkled throughout the day when I can connect with God if and when I choose to do so. He is faithful; he is always there, just waiting for me to turn to him. These small pockets of time have become like an oasis for my parched, landlocked soul.

Now, I know you're probably tired and overextended like I am—maybe even more so! Carving out time for quiet prayer and meditation can make climbing Mount Everest sound like a walk in the park, especially when you have little ones or children with special needs. But I would argue that the more demanding your vocation, the more necessary this time with the Lord becomes. We've all heard that we can't give what we don't have—that we must put an oxygen mask on ourselves before helping someone else with theirs. Being a mom at peace has to be a choice I make, a resolution I keep, a state of mind, body, and soul I choose to cultivate through habit and intention, just as if I were tending a fragile garden. Is it simple? Yes. Is it easy? No way! I try and fail, and try and fail, and try and fail again. When I succeed, through the grace of God and the outpouring of the Holy Spirit, is it worth the effort I made? Abso-freaking-lutely. I'm calmer, less reactionary, and don't fly off the handle in anger and frustration nearly as often as I did before I learned how to make friends with the silence. I've found that, in God's economy, every attempt I make to turn to him multiplies my peace and divides my anxiety.

There's a story about Saint Francis de Sales and Saint Jane Francis de Chantal, who were fighting for reform in their religious order. Saint Francis remained as calm as a cucumber, while Saint Jane grew more and more agitated, until she asked Saint Francis, "Why don't you get more upset?"

He replied: "My child. I have spent over thirty years

working toward inner peace. Do you think I am going to give that up so easily?"

Call me a crazy hippie, but I truly believe that peace—in my heart, in my marriage, with my children, in my life—begins within me. I've experienced how it trickles down from an outpouring in my soul, touching those I encounter and effecting calm. Conversely, when I am *not* at peace, my children pick up on it. Even my *dog* picks up on it. But c'mon, guys—I'm human. Things agitate me. I *do* get upset. Like Mother Angelica said, "If it wasn't for people, we could all be holy." I just try really hard not to allow those things, noisy children in the minivan included, to steal my peace. I have to persistently *choose* to be at peace, rather than allow things to bother me.

I still struggle with internal noise, too. When my efforts to quiet the swinging monkey troop fail, I know it's time to hit the adoration chapel and/or the confessional for a spiritual tuneup. By doing so, I'm telling external noise and chaos that there's no room for them to park in my garage or in front of my house or even around the block. I'm not giving the external noise and chaos permission to rule my life. I can't often control what happens around me, but I can control my response. Or, you know, I *should* be able to. More about that in another chapter.

● ● ●

Roadblocks to peace

Finding and keeping peace in our daily lives can sometimes seem completely unattainable—but it can be done, if we're willing to work around some of the obstacles we encounter. Here are a few nuggets I picked up from my time in silent retreat:

Noise: The world is noisy. So is my brain—and probably yours, too. But God is present *in the silence.* If we don't allow silence on the outside, it is much, much more difficult to hear God's voice on the inside. In the silence, your heart and soul can be nourished in ways you didn't know you were hungering for. Granted, absence of noise does not necessarily mean you're internally peaceful. It takes practice, which takes time and discipline. Be patient with yourself. Even the great mystics and parents of the Church had to work at cultivating silence!

I encourage you to turn off the extra noise whenever you can and let God speak to you in the silence. Don't fill every moment with extra noise just because it's what you're used to. Making time for silence takes discipline, but so does making dinner for your family, or brushing your teeth, or getting out of bed, or going to Mass. Seeking the Lord in the quiet is a wonderful gift to give yourself (and it spreads to your family and friends!), even if it's just in little pockets throughout the day.

Neglecting prayer: I remember when I was a young mom who wanted to grow in holiness, but lamented, "I just don't have *time* for prayer!" And, truly, between the feeding, bathing, cleaning, and all other *-ings* motherhood entails, I genuinely believed I *didn't* have time. Even attending Mass on Sunday didn't feel very prayerful, what with wrangling needy littles and taking multiple trips to the restroom. Eventually, though, I wondered: what sort of a relationship can I have with someone for whom I don't make time? What would my relationship with my husband or children be like if I always told them I didn't have time for them? I mean, even *Jesus* went away to be alone with his heavenly Father and pray! Feeling convicted, I began slowly by praying a daily Morning Offering right after my alarm went off. This prayer recognizes that everything I do throughout the day can be a prayer, if freely offered to the Lord with love.

Over the years, at various times I've incorporated the Rosary, Scripture study, the Divine Mercy Chaplet, and various novenas in addition to times of meditation and silence.

I've been known to pray these prayers early in the morning or late at night; while feeding babies, doing dishes, folding laundry; and, yes, in the minivan. I've also taken Saint Augustine's advice to heart, singing praise and worship songs and hymns so I can "pray twice."

During the busiest of seasons in family life, when pockets of personal prayer time are few and far between, I still endeavor to maintain a running conversation with the Lord by offering "arrow prayers" ("Praise God!" or "Help me, Jesus!") . throughout the day. I've found that, in God's economy, when I order my day by prioritizing time with him, my energy and capacity for getting things done is multiplied. I can't tell you exactly how it works; I can only tell you that it does.

Constant talking: When you're on silent retreat and the only words you say out loud are prayers, you realize that many words you speak aren't actually necessary. Maybe we'd have more peace in our lives if the words we chose to speak were an improvement over silence. I'm still working on this one.

Lack (and even fear) of solitude: Being alone can be scary, but it's also an amazing time of self-discovery. And there's no need to be afraid, because when you are alone, you're never *really* alone. God is with you, even in the solitude. I took Father Dave Pivonka's book *Spiritual Freedom* with me into my times of private study on retreat and would recommend it to anyone seeking a closer relationship with Christ.

Busy family life: Believe it or not, it's possible to experience great peace even when you're managing a boisterous household or navigating an acute crisis.

Ultimately, inner peace is contentment resulting from the awareness that we're always in the presence of our loving God, held and protected in his hand. This peace is truly that which surpasses understanding. It is the peace the world cannot give. No one—not crying babies, nor whiny toddlers, nor argumentative teens—can take this peace away from you unless you choose to give it away. Oh, and by the way—believe it or not—I have attended quite a few more silent retreats since that initial experience. Being tricked by a joyful, mischievous Filipino nun and her Honey is one of the best things to happen to me. Rest assured that, if I can survive a silent retreat, you can, too. Pinky promise.

• • •

Yield to the power of the Holy Spirit
(prayer)

Dear Jesus,
Help me to understand that you created me as a human *being*, not a human *doing*. While there's nothing wrong with tasks and activity, I also need time to be still and know that you are God. Help me to quiet my heart, body, and mind so that I can hear the still, small sound of your voice.

Come, Holy Spirit—fill me with your peace. Amen.

• • •

GPS: God Positioning System
(scripture)

"Be still and know that I am God.
I am exalted among the nations,
I am exalted in the earth!" — Psalms 46:10

"Peace I leave with you; my peace I give to you; not as the world gives do I give to you. Let not your hearts be troubled, neither let them be afraid." — John 14:27

"Have no anxiety about anything, but in everything by prayer and supplication with thanksgiving let your requests

be made known to God. And the peace of God, which pass-
es all understanding, will keep your hearts and your minds
in Christ Jesus." — Philippians 4:6–7

"I have said this to you, that in me you may have peace. In
the world you have tribulation; but be of good cheer, I have
overcome the world." — John 16:33

"And let the peace of Christ rule in your hearts, to which
indeed you were called in the one body. And be thankful."
— Colossians 3:15

"And he said to them, 'Come away by yourselves to a lonely
place, and rest a while.' For many were coming and going, .
and they had no leisure even to eat." — Mark 6:31

"Cast all your anxieties on him, for he cares about you."
— 1 Peter 5:7

"May the LORD give strength to his people!
May the LORD bless his people with peace!" — Psalms 29:11

"For the mountains may depart
and the hills be removed,
but my mercy shall not depart from you,
and my covenant of peace shall not be removed,
says the LORD, who has compassion on you." — Isaiah 54:10

"Come to me, all who labor and are heavy laden, and I will
give you rest. Take my yoke upon you, and learn from me;
for I am gentle and lowly in heart, and you will find rest for
your souls. For my yoke is easy, and my burden is light."
— Matthew 11:28–30

"Now may the Lord of peace himself give you peace at all
times in all ways. The Lord be with you all."
— 2 Thessalonians 3:16

• • •

Roadside Assistance

(wisdom from the saints and others)

"All shall be well and all shall be well and all manner of thing shall be well." — Julian of Norwich

"Pray, hope, and don't worry. Worry is useless. God is merciful and will hear your prayer." — Saint Padre Pio

"Make me an instrument of your peace."
— Saint Francis of Assisi

"Our hearts were made for you, O Lord, and they are restless until they rest in thee." — Saint Augustine

"Let us go forward in peace, our eyes upon heaven, the only one goal of our labors." — Saint Thérèse of Lisieux

• • •

Pit Stop

(other resources)

- Read *The Way of the Heart* by Henri Nouwen. It's a poignant text pulling from the wisdom of Scripture and the Desert Fathers to draw us into a deeper connection with God, who waits for us in the silence.

- Read *Searching for and Maintaining Peace* by Father Jacques Philippe. It is the absolute best book I've ever read on the topic. It's short, sweet, and to the point— just what we busy moms need! If you haven't read it yet, please put this book down right now and go order it. It's that good. I think I've recommended and given it away more than any other title I've read. If you get absolutely nothing from reading it, please send me your copy; I will find it a good home!

- Join or create a moms child-care co-op through your parish, school, or with a few friends. Here's the idea: mom members take turns watching one another's children on a rotating basis so the other members have an hour or two to themselves. Rather than spending the whole time running errands or doing chores, carve out time for kid-free confession, quiet meditation and prayer, or good, old-fashioned *rest*.

- Listen to Gregorian chant—an ancient form of musical prayer from the early Church that soothes the soul. There are many different options available for free online.

- Make a holy hour (or quarter-hour, or half-hour) at your local church or adoration chapel. Check out www.mass-times.org for locations.

- Sign up for a retreat at a local retreat house, either with a group or on your own. Some retreat houses, like the one I frequent, even welcome nursing babies! Bonus points if you remain silent the entire time!

● ● ●

Your Ideas

_____

_____

_____

_____

• • •

Discuss Amongst Yourselves
(questions)

1.   What is the peace the world cannot give?

2.   Moms are very busy people. How do we take the time to be still and know that he is God?

3.   Consider one practical way you will work to add more peace, quiet, and prayer to your life this week.

ARE WE THERE YET??

((patience))

*"Patience: What you have when there are
too many witnesses."*

— *Unknown*

• • •

Small red grocery basket overflowing, my youngest child and I headed toward the checkout lanes. Since all the self-serve stations were occupied, we high-tailed it to the nearest open lane. *What a blessing!* I thought. *There's no one else in line!* I figured we'd be out of there in no time flat, and move on to the next four kajillion things I needed to do that day.

Perhaps the lack of cashier stationed at the register should have been my first clue. But the light above the checkout lane appeared illuminated, so I began unloading our groceries. Since we didn't have too many items, I figured my patience could endure while Kolbe, ever the helpful assistant, pitched in as only dear preschoolers can: sloooowly. Once everything was on the conveyor belt, I wondered why no cashier was there to assist us yet.

After an awkward minute or two, I signaled an employee and asked if someone could please help us on lane 14. It was as the employee said, *"Ma'am, lane 14 isn't open,"* that I realized the iridescent sign above me wasn't, in actuality, *on.*

"Oh!" I exclaimed, embarrassed by my oversight. "I thought the light was lit!"

The employee nodded. "Sure; that happens a lot," he said. "People see the reflection from the light of the self-serve stations and think number 14 is open, but it isn't."

I could have sworn I heard the intercom blaze to life at that moment with a bored, yet slightly amused voice bellowing: "Can we get a wake-up call for the doofus, er, customer on lane 14? Wake-up call on lane 14."

Well, *gee whiz.* I laughed self-consciously as I rushed to put our items back in the basket and ushered my young son away from treacherous, no good, lying lane 14. *Here again,* I thought, *is an example of why I don't need to pray for humility; I am perfectly capable of humiliating myself all on my own, thank you very much!*

In total, my misperception and impulsivity cost us a scant eight extra minutes of our day. And yet, with that stupid mistake breathing down my neck and my to-do list jeering at me from my purse, it felt like we'd fallen at least two hours behind schedule. Exasperated, I searched and found a checkout lane that was actually open with a real, live cashier assisting flesh-and-blood customers under the glow of an honest-to-goodness illuminated lane light.

I found myself gritting my teeth as if in physical duress while Kolbe and I worked again to unload … our … twelve … items.

"You have quite the good little helper there," the cashier said with a cheery voice, indicating my son. I looked over at Kolbe, who, task completed, was happily investigating the candy bars near the register. The cashier's comment smacked me across the face as I realized that, yes—yes, he *was* a good helper. *He* wasn't throwing an internal fit over unloading boxes of cereal and milk and applesauce on the wrong conveyor belt and having to reload them in the basket and unload them again; that was all me.

And what did I really have to get done that day, anyway? I'd just submitted an assignment for work, so I didn't have to rush home to my laptop. I didn't need to pick up anybody from school for several hours. Most of the four kajillion things that I thought I needed to do so urgently, when reconsidered, weren't really so urgent. I mean, we had to go home, unpack groceries, get Kolbe a snack, let the dog out, and throw another load of laundry in the wash eventually, but the other things? They could wait.

Kolbe looked up at me and smiled as he showed me the sticker the cashier had given him. And I slowed my roll long enough to genuinely smile back at him.

This whole situation made me think: how often do I hurriedly press forward, full-steam ahead, in what I *think* is the right direction, only to discover down the road that my inner compass isn't calibrated correctly, and I've completely missed my exit? I had been so intent on plowing through my agenda that I nearly missed my son's helpfulness, the cashier's kindness, and who knows what else.

During my years away from the Church, I pretty much threw away my God Positioning System. I wasn't talking to God much, and I was pretty sure he wasn't interested in talking to me. I figured I knew where I wanted to go and could get there on my own. Eventually, and in an enormous amount of pain, I finally admitted that I was so totally off the beaten path that I couldn't even find a map, let alone follow it. Slowly yet surely, through the mercy of God and the graces of sacramental life, I was able to change my course and get back on the narrow way—the path of life.

Since then, I've found it can be most painful to change my plans when I'm convinced a fragrant paradise awaits if I can *just keep driving as fast as I can. I just want to get there. Somewhere. Anywhere. Just not here.* For example: things would just be so much better if we had a bigger house. Or a better car. Or a nicer yard. Or better weather. Or money for summer camp. *Are we there yet? Are we there yet? Are we there yet?* The truth remains: persistently driving as fast as I can in the wrong direction is just being persistently wrong *more quickly.*

Often, I fall prey to smaller navigational errors. I adopt behaviors and take on tasks without a second thought, determining they're harmless—good, even. I don't slow down long enough to really consider the consequences of my actions. I want to be a "yes" person. I want to help. I want to please. And there's probably a part of me that's afraid I'll miss out on something important if I don't jump into the fray. Right! Now! *Why shouldn't I volunteer to run the school such-and-so?* I ask myself, overlooking that the such-and-so conflicts with the this, that, and the other I already said I'd do. I forge ahead along a path of my own design, adding items to my basket, feeling accomplished, eventually showing them to God and asking him to check me out—even if they're not things he's calling me to do; even if they're not things that will ultimately make life better for my family or the people I care about.

During these detours, I wonder if God smiles at me the same way I used to smile at my daughter when she put her socks on inside out: *I love the effort, Sweetheart. You're not quite there yet, but you sure are trying, aren't you?*

After the grocery store incident, I'm wondering what life would look like if, instead of barreling ahead with tunnel vision, impatiently flying from thing to thing, I stopped for a moment. What if, instead of rushing toward the light I think I can see, I asked God to help me see things with his eyes? What would happen if I slowed my roll long enough to confirm that where I'm headed is where he's leading me, leading my children? What if I conferred with the Master Mapmaker instead of piecing together my own route, blinded and broken as I am? What if I took the time to wait ... on the *Lord*?

The waiting is the hardest part

In case you couldn't tell by now, I am not, by nature, a particularly patient person. From an early age, waiting felt like an agonizing torment. When I was little, I couldn't wait to go to school. Once I was in school, I couldn't wait to be an adult. Once I was an adult, I couldn't wait to get married. Once we had kids, I couldn't wait to get a decent night's sleep again, or for the toddler to be potty-trained. As a writer, I couldn't wait to finish this book. You get the picture.

I'd like to think that all this "can't wait" business is merely a sign of my zest for life—my excitement about existence and the adventure around the bend. Yet if I'm honest, it is usually more about lack of appreciation for where God has me in life right now, an internal restlessness and insatiability. "Bloom where you're planted" makes for a swell phrase on a bumper sticker, but it's probably meant to be on someone else's car. I figure I'll bloom when I get there. Except, once I arrive, *if* I arrive, there's often somewhere else I think I need to be.

Now, I don't have to tell you that motherhood requires a boatload of patience. And we aren't talking a one-person, kayak-sized boat, either. More like a barge, attached to forty-nine of his best barge buddies besides. Approximately seventeen-and-a-half hours of your day just might be spent waiting for other people to get their rears in gear. You wait for kids to find (matching) shoes and coats that have inexplicably disappeared in the two minutes since anyone saw them last. You wait for someone to finish on the potty, and then the next one has to go. You wait for someone to make eye contact so you know she hears your words regarding that chore she "forgot" to do. You wait for someone to stop whining so you can explain why putting Legos in the microwave is a bad idea. And then there's the time you spend waiting at doctor appointments, sports practices, school or church events, for someone to eat their vegetables, for another person to get a clue … the list is endless.

With apologies to Thomas Paine, *these* are the times that try mamas' souls. Meanwhile, I'm still waiting for the magi-

cal fountain that gushes forth with an infinite supply of patience to arrive on my doorstep.

Still, I've found that, like most things worth doing, *practicing* patience with my children helps me *be* more patient
with my children. It's not enough just to worry about it or
talk about it; I have to make the decision to do it.

The problem is, while I think I'm getting better at being more patient with my children, my improvement often
doesn't happen quickly enough for my taste. Why can't I just
accept that we have to allow at *least* five minutes per child
and per pet before we have to be out the door? Why am I not
okay with the fact that we can't change plans on a dime like
other families I know? Are we there yet? Are we there yet?
Are we there yet?? Do you see the irony? I am pretty darn
impatient with *myself.*

A wise priest suggested I look into the writings of Saint
Francis de Sales. And I must say—Francis was a genius. He
said: "Have patience with all things, but chiefly have patience
with yourself. Do not lose courage in considering your own
imperfections but instantly set about remedying them—every day begin the task anew."

You'll notice he didn't say we should instantly chastise
and flog ourselves for our imperfections; rather, we should
"instantly set about remedying them." That's an important
difference. As Flannery O'Connor said, "Accepting oneself
does not preclude an attempt to become better." So, I can
love myself despite my natural proclivity to rush into things,
all while working on slowing down and cultivating patience
with others as well as myself.

Patience with others, especially my children, has a lot
to do, I think, with recognizing their strengths and weaknesses. For example, I wouldn't expect the preschooler to
help tie the teenager's shoes, but I can expect that sort of
help from my teen. Accepting and loving my kiddos for
who they are *right now* while gently encouraging them to
gain the skills they need for later in life is a huge part of my
calling. Now, when the baby poops as we're walking out the

door (and he *always* poops as we're walking out the door), pretty much all bets are off.

Being more patient with myself, I think, begins by recalling how incredibly patient God has been with me. I mean, much of my life has surely been one continuous face palm or headdesk for the Man Upstairs, yet he patiently waits for me to reroute and get back on track. Surely, as I'm harnessing just a small bit of that supernatural patience for my spouse and my children, I can allow a little for myself as well.

● ● ●

Roadblocks to patience

I think for many of us, lack of patience is often rooted in the same things.

Pride: Deep down, perhaps I believe my tasks, agenda, and timeline supersede anyone else's (including God's). And I don't think I'm alone in this. Mother Angelica said, "Patience is adjusting your time to God's time." And Saint Padre Pio said, "You can't give God deadlines." Apparently, you also can't give deadlines to a preschooler who refuses to buckle her car seat. I mean, you can *try*, but in my experience, it doesn't usually work out so well.

I'm sorry to say that, in times past (and occasionally in times present—hey, I'm no saint yet!) I've yelled and threatened when children's responses to my requests didn't align with my time frame. Funny thing, though—my raging mommy antics don't often convince my kid to do what I want him to do when I want it done. And I end up drowning my sorrows in an iced coffee and direct messages to my girlfriends about what a horrible parent I am.

Selfishness: We human beings want what we want when we want it. Living in a high-speed, drive-through, ATM culture doesn't help matters much. Instant gratification is a golden calf to which many of us pay unwitting homage.

Distrust: I don't know about you, but I don't always trust that everything will be okay if it doesn't happen when and how I think it should.

If you're a word nerd like me, you'll be interested to know that the root of the word patience is *pati*, which comes from the Latin word *patientia*, which means "suffering." Aha! So, I was right all those years ago—having to be patient *is* agonizing! But how did Christ suffer? With humility. With meekness. With grace. And only by the power of the Holy Spirit can we suffer through some of the many speed bumps the highway of life puts in our path with patience, humility, and grace, so long as God is there to guide us.

Jesus, I trust in you!

(By the way, my computer inexplicably shut down five different times while I was writing this chapter. And, based on my response to *that* fiasco, I know that God isn't done with me quite yet. Good thing he's so patient.)

• • •

Yield to the power of the Holy Spirit
(prayer)

Dear heavenly Father,
You alone know how incredibly impatient I can be sometimes, both with my children and with myself. I don't always see where things are headed for me and my family, or how you're leading us. I don't always trust that your timing is not only better than mine, but that it's perfect. Dear God, please help me to wait on you, conforming my will to your will and my time to yours. Help me to be as patient in times of waiting as you have been with me.

Come, Holy Spirit—fill me with your patience. Amen.

• • •

GPS: God Positioning System

(scripture)

"Wait for the LORD;
be strong, and let your heart take courage;
yes, wait for the LORD!" — Psalms 27:14

"The LORD is merciful and gracious,
slow to anger and abounding in mercy." — Psalms 103:8

"But they who wait for the LORD shall renew their strength;
they shall mount up with wings like eagles,
they shall run and not be weary,
they shall walk and not faint." — Isaiah 40:31

"Rejoice in your hope, be patient in tribulation, be constant
in prayer." — Romans 12:12

"For still the vision awaits its time;
it hastens to the end—it will not lie.
If it seem slow, wait for it;
it will surely come, it will not delay." — Habakkuk 2:3

• • •

Roadside Assistance

(wisdom from the saints and others)

"Let nothing disturb you,
Let nothing frighten you,
All things are passing away:
God never changes.
Patience obtains all things.
Whoever has God lacks nothing;
God alone suffices." — Saint Teresa of Ávila

"Patience, prayer, and silence—these are what give strength to the soul." — Saint Faustina Kowalska

"Continue to be patient; it will all be for your good."
— Saint Padre Pio

● ● ●

Pit Stop
(other resources)

- Take a field trip to your local nursery. Select seeds for something to plant with your children. Observe the various changes as you tend your plant, and watch your patience grow along with it.

- Visit an elderly person in your life. If you don't know any senior citizens, call a local care facility and ask to visit the person who needs it most. Take the time to sit with them, listen to their stories, or play a game.

- Practice delayed gratification the next time you're tempted to purchase something, whether it's as small as a coffee or as large as a sofa. Consider the benefits of denying yourself for a time.

- The next time you're stuck in traffic or waiting on a slow-poke family member, say a prayer asking the Holy Spirit to grant you the patience you need to persevere in love.

• • •

Your Ideas

_____

_____

_____

_____

_____

• • •

Discuss Amongst Yourselves
(questions)

1. Consider the last time you struggled to be patient with your child(ren) ... or yourself. How did you handle the situation, and what would you do, if anything, to improve your response?

2. What does "waiting on the Lord" mean to you, especially as it relates to raising your family?

3. This week, what practical steps can you take to be more patient with your loved ones and yourself?

FOOT OFF THE GAS

((gentleness))

"Life, deal gently with her ... Love, never desert her."
— *Lucy Maud Montgomery*

• • •

When you hear the word "gentle," what comes to mind? Your childhood blankie or favorite stuffed toy? Maybe you think about the lullabies your mom sang to you at bedtime, or the pillow-soft feel of pussy willow blossoms against your cheek. The first thing that pops into my head is the song "Hail Mary, Gentle Woman" by Reverend Carey Landry. *Thanks, Catholic school Mass.* Seriously, though, I think it's natural to think of Mary when considering gentleness, don't you? All those thousands of depictions of our Blessed Mother, serenely holding her divine Son, looking preternaturally peaceful and super-duper holy.

I can imagine Our Lady humming sweetly as she sweeps the floor of the Holy Family's house, young Jesus crawling on the floor, putting his hands in the dirt and laughing. Mary gently wipes his hands clean, redirecting him to another area while she patiently sweeps up the same desert dirt for the third or fourth time. I'm so gratefully glad the role of the Mother of God was already taken by the Blessed Virgin Mary. Because I could never, ever in an infinity plus googol-plex years hope to fill her sandals—be that trusting, generous, kind, loving, and gentle.

Some moms seem to have a real knack for gentleness, but not all of us are wired that way. I don't know about you, but for me, sustained gentleness can be achieved only with great effort and internal consternation. Like so many things, being gentle is a choice—an act of the will.

We have a child who notoriously refused to remain buckled in her car seat when she was little. The school-aged kids would jump in the van after school, ready to go home for the day, and without fail, this little gal would find a way to unfasten her seatbelt despite my expectations, instructions, and admonitions for her to keep it *on*. After several incidents, I was done with my otherwise sweet daughter hijacking our afternoons with her seatbelt shenanigans. I decided I didn't want to yell, threaten, or bribe her into compliance anymore. So, one day, after my beltless wonder did her thing yet again, I silently asked the Blessed Virgin Mary to please give me just one *smidgen* of her gentleness so I wouldn't completely lose it with my kid who was frustrating the heck out of me.

As I got out of my seat and opened the sliding door to the van, I prayed aloud: "Hail Mary, full of grace, the Lord is with thee." The older kids looked at me incredulously, like, "Mom, what are you DOING?" I continued calmly, as I moved closer to my daughter, who was standing next to her younger brother: "Blessed art thou among women, and blessed is the fruit of thy womb, Jesus." At this point, my youngest girl was looking directly at me with her twinkly brown eyes and, to my surprise, joined in: "Hoewee Mehwee, muhvuh uhv God, pway foe us sinuhhz …" and I held out my hand to her, guiding her back to her seat as we finished: "now and at the hour of our death. Amen." And without another word, she sat down in her seat and allowed me to buckle her up.

I wish I could say I wasn't shocked that my desperate prayer strategy worked, but ... I was. I'd never tried doing something like that before. The funny thing was, on the rare occasion when Gigi would attempt a repeat performance with her seatbelt, I'd make eye contact with her in the rear-view mirror and say, "Hail Mary ... " and she would immediately put her belt back on. I'm still not sure this is the correct way to teach children their prayers, but it definitely worked for us.

Physical gentleness came easily to me early in my new motherhood, but in hindsight maybe that's because I was terrified of dropping or squishing or breaking Ava, our baby daughter. Such a sweet new soul, a huge piece of my heart just lying there, outside of my body, wrapped in a blanket burrito in the hospital bassinet. All those tiny yet perfectly formed fingers and toes. And that head—that soft, fragile, glorious-smelling head—it was mysterious and wonderful, and I was completely overwhelmed.

Then, a couple of years ago, we entered into unknown territory: adolescence. And poof! Just like the twelve candles blown out on her cake, everything I knew about interacting with my first baby vanished. My efforts to be gentle with her were met with indifference, resistance, and outright rejection. I felt entirely out of my depths. Nothing seemed to be getting through.

One day, Ava seemed really upset. She often keeps her problems to herself, so despite being dog tired from the rigmarole of the day, I invited her to come talk in our room after the younger kids went to bed. As thing after thing after thing spilled out from her heart, I wanted to help, to fix it, to console her in some way. And she wasn't having it. She was disappointed and angry, and she wept bitter tears with an intensity and quantity I had never seen before. As she continued to reject my numerous attempts to console her, however, I found myself getting more and more agitated, tempted to anger and impatience. I was tired. I was *really* trying. Yet things that had worked to calm her before (and still worked with her younger siblings), like holding hands, giving hugs, offering reassuring words, or singing lullabies—none of these things seemed to be what she needed. So I decided to stop trying to *do* anything and I just … sat with her. I stayed as close to her as she would allow while she cried.

Soon, I was crying, too. It is so hard on a mama's heart to see her child suffering, and it can be even more difficult, knowing that a "wambaid" (my kids' word for a bandage) can't fix things. There was no visible boo-boo to kiss and make better. There was no medicine that would quell this deep hurt of her heart. All I could do was be present, silently praying that God would help me bring her comfort, to be the love that she so desperately needed.

After many minutes, my beloved firstborn was receptive to my offer of a tissue, and then a word or two of comfort. And then a glass of water. And then more words, offered quietly and humbly. I spoke the truth about who she was in a way that was different than I had when she was younger. She was growing and changing, and apparently she needed me to grow and change, too.

The Blessed Mother takes me to school

Eventually the time for sleep came, and my girl accepted a half hug and a blessing before heading to her room downstairs. I sighed as I closed the door, wondering and worrying if I had done anything of worth—anything of value—for this burgeoning young lady, who felt things so deeply and seemed to need me so very little most days. As I lay my head on my pillow, I began to pray the Sorrowful Mysteries of the Rosary.

I'm not exactly sure why I chose to pray the Sorrowful Mysteries that night, except that I felt sad that my daughter was hurting. Uniting my sorrow with Jesus' passion seemed fitting. The significance of the tremendous anguish our Blessed Mother endured as she watched her child suffer was not lost on me as I prayed. The Holy Spirit began to show me that in sitting, staying, and being watchful, I was actually practicing the truest form of gentleness.

Mary couldn't make Jesus' pain go away. All she could do was stay as close to him as possible. Although Scripture doesn't mention it, there is a tradition that Mary suffered every part of Jesus' passion with him, although from a distance. While the disciples fell asleep during Jesus' agony in the garden, I'd bet anything that Mary stayed wide awake. Like Mary, while I couldn't remove the pain, I could choose to stay awake with and pray for my dear child.

There's a scene in Mel Gibson's movie *The Passion of the Christ*, after the horrible scourging at the pillar: Mary could not save Jesus from being tortured, couldn't comfort him in his excruciating pain or dress his wounds, but afterward she stayed to mop up his precious blood. His blood was not nothing, to be left to seep into the earth; this was a sacred sacrifice, meant to cover the sins of the whole world.

On the Way of the Cross, Mary followed her beloved Jesus, watched him fall under the unbearable weight of the cross, fall to his knees, face hitting the dusty road. She couldn't run to him or comfort him in her arms and make the pain disappear as she must have done when he was a child. All she could do now was stay with him as he continued on to the place where he would be killed. And so she did.

Jesus was crucified. And Mary was there. Praying. Present. Sitting at the foot of the cross with him. She could do nothing more than that, but it was enough. And a sword pierced her heart.

Gentleness isn't always what we picture—it isn't necessarily love in action, like kindness (more on that in another chapter), but it also isn't passive. More than anything else, gentleness is choosing to be docile to the Holy Spirit, asking what he wants of us in each new circumstance and obeying, just as our Blessed Mother did. Sometimes I want to be Mama Bear, saving and protecting my kids from suffering and sadness. And, of course, one of a mother's many jobs is to protect her children as best she can, especially when they are little. I've found, though, that many times what they really need is for me to simply be present to them, respecting where they are and the needs they have. Forcing my own desire to help or console or fix upon these young souls isn't gentle—it's actually quite selfish and prideful. Gentleness recognizes the dignity, the inherent worth of the other, and allows that to inform our actions.

Reflecting on the Sorrowful Mysteries with the Blessed Mother, it hit me: in my attempts to care for my daughter, I was doing what I could do. And that, through the grace of the Holy Spirit, was enough.

When practicing gentleness, remember to include yourself

As it turns out, I wasn't being very gentle with myself about how I'd handled this situation. I was having a hard time accepting that anything I had done was helpful to my sweet girl. I was beating myself up for not being able to do much, for not being able to fix it. But maybe that wasn't the point.

We strive and we endeavor and we try to do and be and have and make everything beautiful and edifying for our kids. Even if we get some things right, we can still feel like we are failing, and we criticize ourselves when, really, what our kids want most is our loving presence. They need to be assured that, like the Blessed Mother, we're not going anywhere. That's gentleness.

How can we do it, sisters? How can we be as gentle with ourselves as we want to be with our children? How can we remember that we, too, are children with a heavenly Father who is gentle with us? He sends his Holy Spirit like a balm to comfort, inspire, and guide. He allows Mary to be our mother, interceding for us and covering us in her mantle of grace and peace. Perhaps gentleness with ourselves begins when we remember who we are and who God is, when we trust that we are his, that he loves us more than we can possibly imagine, and that his love will never change. Maybe it starts when we stop trying so hard and realize that what we need has been right there, all along, in our midst. He is Emmanuel—God with us.

• • •

Roadblocks to gentleness

Anger: It's impossible to be gentle when we're acting like a raging lunatic. Gentleness takes a moment, breathes deeply, chooses not to react out of anger, and moves forward in love.

Impulsivity: Do you ever act or speak before you think? Yeah, me neither. Ha, ha. Gentleness isn't about jumping into the melee without thinking. It takes time to consider its options, then gracefully chooses the one closest to reflecting the image and likeness of God.

Harshness or loudness: Gentleness would never think of raising its voice or uttering a harsh word. Rather, it is bathed in love and baptized in peace. Gentleness is kind and temperate.

Agitation/irritability: When we're all twisted up about what someone has said or done, how we've failed, or even a particularly troubling circumstance, we cannot manifest the fruit of gentleness to our family and friends. Ask the Holy Spirit to help you attain *his* peace so that you are supernaturally equipped to treat those around you (and yourself) with gentleness.

• • •

Yield to the power of the Holy Spirit
(prayer)

Dear Jesus,
Help me to be a wife and mother after your Blessed Mother's Immaculate Heart. I know that it is through my gen-

tleness that your love and mercy are shown. Give me the strength I need to be truly gentle with those entrusted to my care as well as with myself. Lord, I want to be gentle as your Blessed Mother is gentle, completely trusting in your love to guide me and those I love on the path of life.

Come, Holy Spirit—fill me with your gentleness. Amen.

• • •

GPS: God Positioning System
(scripture)

"A gentle tongue is a tree of life." — Proverbs 15:4

"And the Lord's servant must not be quarrelsome but kindly to every one, an apt teacher, forbearing, correcting his opponents with gentleness." — 2 Timothy 2:24–25

"A soft answer turns away wrath, but a harsh word stirs up anger." — Proverbs 15:1

"Take my yoke upon you, and learn from me; for I am gentle and lowly in heart, and you will find rest for your souls." — Matthew 11:29

• • •

Roadside Assistance
(wisdom from the saints and others)

"Nothing is so strong as gentleness; nothing is so gentle as real strength." — Saint Francis de Sales

"God rests within gentle hearts. The gentle and merciful shall sit fearless in his regions, and will inherit heavenly glory." — Saint John Climacus

"Just as humility perfects us with respect to God, gentleness perfects us with respect to our neighbor."
— Saint Francis de Sales

"You cannot be too gentle, too kind. Shun even to appear harsh in your treatment of each other."
— Saint Seraphim of Sarov

"It is important to resist evil and address the faults of those placed in our care, and this must be done constantly and courageously, but gently and peacefully." — Saint Francis de Sales

• • •

Pit Stop

(other resources)

- Look into the writings of Saint Francis de Sales. He wrote quite a lot about gentleness, even though he himself struggled with being gentle. His best-known work is the classic *Introduction to the Devout Life*, available online and in public libraries.

- Do you have a baby in your life? If so, observe your behavior the next time you want him or her to go down for a nap. If you don't (and please don't think me crazy), ask a friend if you can come over and help for a bit. Are you jostling the baby or soothing the baby? Are you yelling, or speaking softly (if at all)? What is your body language saying? How is your breathing? Now, the next time someone confronts you with a difficult situation, recall how you acted with that sweet baby. While you needn't rock or sing to or soothe the person with whom you have a conflict, tap into that gentleness and see how the situation resolves itself.

- If you're a particularly reactionary person, begin working on taking a breather between stimulus and response.

For example: your preschooler decides to empty the dog food dish all over the floor. Before responding, so long as there are no safety hazards, take several deep breaths and decide to proceed with gentleness.

• Research articles about "gentle parenting." If you have a chance, read *The Gentle Parent* by L. R. Knost. Consider how the author suggests we can raise our children through gentle discipline.

• • •

Your Ideas

_____

_____

_____

_____

_____

_____

• • •

Discuss Amongst Yourselves

(questions)

1. Consider the gentleness of the Blessed Virgin Mary. How might she influence and inspire you to cultivate the fruit of gentleness in your vocation as wife and mother?

2. Do you recognize your heavenly Father's love for you as gentle? Why or why not?

3. Write down one way you could choose to be more gentle with someone you know this week. Maybe you have a child who challenges your ability to speak calmly, or a colleague who pushes your buttons. What can you do to show that person gentleness, and what fruit do you think it will it bear?

4. Fill in the blank: This week, I will be gentle with myself by _____.

IS IT SUPPOSED TO BE MAKING THAT SOUND?

((humor))

*"No child can resist the power of googly eyes
and a stuck-out tongue."*

— *Amy Poehler*

• • •

There's something you should know: God laughs at me. A lot. It's a wink here, a chuckle there, sometimes an outright guffaw, but I promise he's doing it. And it's fine. I'm okay with it.

Folks are often concerned when I tell them God laughs at me. They try to talk me out of it: "Surely, he isn't laughing *at* you," they'll say, as if it's a bad thing. So I'll share an example of a time when I know he was having a laugh at my expense. And then another. After the fourth or fifth story, they'll concede that perhaps God is laughing *with* me, but *at* me? That just doesn't sound like something the Creator of heaven and earth would do. And yet. Getting a kick out of my silly human folly sounds just like the heavenly Father I know and love. He's not laughing out of malice. It's more akin to the stifled giggle of an amused parent seeing his strong-willed child driving like a maniac at full steam in the wrong direction. He laughs because he knows that, eventually, I'll flip a U-turn, face flushed with a sheepish grin, and drive straight back on the road toward him.

Who are all these children, and why are they calling me Mom?

God's biggest laugh about me, I'm certain, stems from me being a mom. To five children. I mean, this is my life, and it's funny to *me*. For one thing, my birth mother put me up for adoption, as her birth mother did for her. In my lineage, apparently, nobody is equipped to raise a child when they get pregnant the first time. All joking aside, my husband and I each have just one sibling and negligible experience with babies and/or little kids, let alone a whole gaggle of them. Each of our four parents had two siblings apiece. *Other* families were large and in charge—not ours.

Growing up, I could think of a million ways I'd rather earn pocket money than babysitting; I wasn't gaga over babies like some of my friends, but maybe that's because I was traumatized from the time I tried to squeeze my infant cousin into my baby doll carriage to take a stroll around the house, and she wasn't super excited about it. The adults had to rescue her. I still feel bad about that one. (Sorry, Annie.)

Or it could be that, when I was five years old, my parents finally adopted my younger sister. The first time we met, she grabbed a huge handful of my hair, upon which I wailed in response, "Take her back!!"

Fast forward about twenty years, and I met my husband. We fell in love. Quickly. We got engaged, and less than ten months later, we were processing down the aisle of Saint Michael the Archangel Catholic Church in downtown Portland with 250 of our closest friends and family in attendance.

Eventually, we got our acts together regarding the Church's teaching about contraception and natural family planning, and ten months after saying "I do," we were expecting our first bundle of joy.

We were excited and petrified and nervous and amazed. And stunned. Wow. Us. *Parents.*

And then, twenty-one months later, we were expecting again. Another girl. And then, three years later, a boy. And then another girl. And then another boy.

And God certainly must have laughed and laughed and laughed. At least five belly laughs for each of our children and a few "hee hee hoo haw haws" for me and my long-suffering husband. And we kept laughing as much as we could, because we were pretty sure that if we didn't laugh, we could likely spend the next several decades crying or rocking back and forth in a white, padded cell.

David and I wanted to be good Christian parents, so we met with our pastor to see about having our first child baptized. We'd already talked with the individuals we wanted to be godparents, and they'd happily agreed. We made quick work of the baptism prep classes and scheduled our little girl's baptism at our home parish during the 10:45 a.m. Mass.

We should have known that this blessed event wouldn't go down without some sort of excitement, because we invited practically everyone we knew. Despite maintaining the same milk-based diet, our sweet baby hadn't had a dirty diaper in over thirty hours, which was unusual. As first-time parents, we were a little anxious, but we kept hoping things would resolve themselves naturally, so to speak, before Mass began. No such luck. Soon she was dressed in her heirloom baptismal gown and we were off to church, praying that any blowout diaper gremlins would be completely exorcised in anticipation of the sacrament.

It was around the beginning of the Liturgy of the Word when the flatulence began. The sounds were bitty baby-sized at first, barely a blip on the radar. But gradually the toots got bigger and louder, and soon my younger cousins seated in the pew behind us were trying not to laugh during Father's homily. David and I braced ourselves. Once on the altar near the baptismal font, I gingerly handed our darling girl over to her godmother, giving her a look that meant, "Beware! She's ready to blow!" Sure enough, as Father was pouring the holy water over her head and claiming Ava Madeleine for Jesus and his Church, she was completely and thoroughly cleansed, from the inside out. Thankfully, nothing noticeable happened to anyone's clothing, although congregants might have thought us awkwardly giddy parents, what with trying to suppress our giggles and all. Immediately upon completion of the rite, my husband whisked our new little Christian away for a diaper change that, to this day, used an unprecedented number of wet wipes. Sweet Ava became as pure as snow that day. And in the moment of her baptism, praise God, she was truly free indeed.

Of all the things I've lost, I miss my mind the most

Another cause for levity in my house is that I was absent the day God handed out coordination. Whenever I see refined women of recent memory—Grace Kelly, Audrey Hepburn, Ella Fitzgerald, for example—and how they moved through the world with such elegance and lightness of being, I'm quickly reminded that, yep, that elegance thing? I never got it. There's a reason my mom called me *Dunderklumpen* as a child. Coordination is not my charism, but I didn't let that stop me from roller skating into bushes, pitching over skateboards, and wiping out on bicycles. Those activities were fun right until I biffed it, so I kept doing them. As my husband likes to joke, "It's okay to laugh at someone who's hurt, so long as you know it isn't permanent and that it hurts really badly." I still get bruises and have no idea where they came from. I've also been known to fall over without the slightest provocation. I usually blame the lines in the sidewalk or the seams in the carpet for grabbing my ankles.

Any comedian worth his or her joke list knows that pain plus the passage of time equals funny. Personally, I would rather start laughing *while* it hurts, because, why postpone the inevitable? As my favorite childhood author Madeleine L'Engle said, "A good laugh heals a lot of hurts."

I've often believed that the reason I'm so scatterbrained and clumsy is because most of my brain cells got sucked out with the breast milk. Recently, however, I was diagnosed with ADHD, which explains a lot. Regardless of my wonky neuro challenges, humor is one of the healthier ways I cope with things that are hard. And motherhood is often hard for me. Like, stick a red-hot poker in my eye while dancing the conga and hula-hooping hard. So I laugh. A lot. Now, sometimes I laugh before the punch line hits and then even harder once the punch line is delivered. This bothers some people. I admit it can be a bit obnoxious. My sense of humor isn't everyone's cup of sangria, but I'm cool with that. Since I'm the only one who has to live with me 24/7/365, I'll think about changing things up if I start to annoy myself.

But doing life with children in tow is so ridiculous and whimsical and amazing and crazy—I just have to laugh. So I don't cry. And sometimes I still *do* cry, but I would much rather laugh. And so I do. All the time. Just ask my kids. They're right over there, in the corner, pretending they don't know me.

Sometimes my kiddos get in on the jokes, though, much to my delight. The other day, my daughter yelled up from the back of the van: "Mommy! What do you call a boomerang that doesn't come back?" Before I could respond, she shouted, "a stick!" I laughed so hard I almost had to pull over. I'm not really sure why, but that particular joke in that particular moment just tickled my funny bone. God must have known I needed that laugh.

And then my other daughter told me about the guy who walked into a bar. The bartender pointed up at the meat on the ceiling and asked the guy if he'd like to take some home. The guy refused, saying, "The steaks are too high."

Another time, my elementary-aged son randomly piped up from the middle seat after I'd picked him up from school. "Mom," he sighed, "these days I'm just running on Jesus and McDonald's—it's the only way I can survive."

Our youngest daughter frequently talks in her sleep. One morning, her older sister reported that, the night before, Gianna exclaimed: "The laser monkeys are taking over! Hide in your pizza houses!" as well as "Don't let the vegan gorillas kill me!" I promise we haven't been forcing her to watch *Planet of the Apes* or adhere to a strict diet.

This stuff kills me. I love it. Hey, don't judge. It's cheaper than tickets to a comedy club, okay?

Kids say funny things. They *do* funny things. Being around people who say and do funny things can be enormously funny if we allow ourselves to enjoy the lightness and absurdity of the moment.

Moms just want to have fun

Recently, my friend Rachel started posting videos of herself talking to her children, neighbors, and random passersby using a karaoke microphone. She says her son bought it at a yard sale, but she knew fun when she saw it, so she swiped it from him. She and her daughter sang some karaoke together, and then Rachel just kept on singing karaoke by herself. For three hours. Because it was fun. And she could. I asked Rachel about her new pastime. She told me: "It's so easy to forget to have fun when you are a mom. There are so many real issues we have to tackle that we can easily fall into a very intense way of doing business." I couldn't agree more.

There were countless times early on in my motherhood when I simply forgot to enjoy myself. Forgot to laugh. Forgot to enjoy my children or much else, actually. I was taking life (and myself) way too seriously. I forgot that this world isn't my home. Thank God I finally realized that being a mother didn't mean I had to be a humorless, joyless, stick-in-the-mud. Being a good Christian and a good mother doesn't mean I can't dance or sing or laugh my brains out. I can still do all those things—have fun and enjoy life—so long as I remember that there are often ten eyes and ears watching every move I make, for better or worse.

Sometimes I think we forget that holy people can have fun and be funny. Do you think, for example, that Jesus never laughed? I mean, he had the Twelve Apostles to provide him with original material every day for three years. And if you don't think God has a sense of humor, then you obviously haven't seen a platypus. Or a manatee. Or a corpse flower, which can take up to seven years to bloom beautifully yet actually stinks like rotting death. Or heard little kids making toot noises with their armpits. That is the sort of stuff laughs are made of.

If you need permission to let loose, take it from Mother Angelica. "Try to laugh a lot," she said, "because life is funny, and everybody today is too serious. The only tragedy in the world, my friend, is sin."

Speaking of Mother Angelica, if you ever need some levity in your life, go online and find a video called "Watch Mother Angelica Have a Laugh Attack Over One of Her Own Jokes." I dare you not to chuckle, if just a little. And I defy anyone to say that Mother wasn't a holy woman. Even Saint Thomas Aquinas, Doctor of the Church and author of enormous theological tomes, said, "It is requisite for the relaxation of the mind that we make use, from time to time, of playful deeds and jokes."

The other day I was distracted and in such a hurry that I didn't realize I'd put on my pants *inside out* until I was dropping the kids off at school. I thought something felt slightly off when I put them on, but evidently it wasn't weird enough to get me to stop and investigate before leaving the house. Once I figured out what I'd done, I started laughing. One of my daughters asked what was so funny, so I told her I was laughing at myself for putting my pants on wrong. She was worried. "Mom," she said, "you shouldn't laugh at yourself!" I quickly enlightened her on the finer points of self-deprecating humor and promised her I don't actually hate myself.

Not even a little. Life is just extraordinarily bonkers much of the time. Besides, why should everyone else get all the laughs? My pants want in on it, too.

Now, cultivating a sense of humor doesn't mean you're going to start telling knock-knock jokes to the ushers after Mass on Sunday. It also doesn't necessarily mean you've got to grab a microphone and let the good times roll like my friend Rachel. It doesn't mean that there aren't times when we must be serious, or firm, or even grieving (see Eccl 3:1–8). What cultivating a sense of humor does mean is laughing more easily at yourself, recognizing the lighter moments in life, and sharing some silliness and fun with your children. As renowned Catholic theologian and scholar Dr. Peter Kreeft said: "Don't be more serious than God. God invented dog farts. God designed your body's plumbing system. God designed an ostrich." Anyone who made those things surely must have wanted us to giggle, if only a little.

If my children learn anything from me, I hope they learn to take loving God and neighbor seriously, and themselves much, much less so. G. K. Chesterton famously said, "Angels can fly because they take themselves lightly." I don't know about you, but if given the choice between flying and being a sour-faced stick-in-the-mud, I'd much rather fly.

● ● ●

Roadblocks to developing a sense of humor

Exhaustion: Wanna hear a joke? What did the tired mom say to the other tired mom? Zzzzzzzzzzz. Who wants to crack jokes when their eyelids are dragging on the dining room table? Sometimes, though, a good belly laugh goes a long way in rejuvenating the spirit and awakening the mind. Try it before you knock (knock) it!

Not feelin' it: When we're upset, angry, afraid, or sad, it can be difficult to laugh about what's happening in our lives.

That might mean it's time to call your funniest friend and see whether he or she can cheer you up. You know what they say, right? Laughter is the best medicine. Drink up.

People-pleasing: If you've ever wondered what people would think if you told a joke that bombed, or laughed at something so hard that everyone at the next booth in the restaurant threatened to get up and leave, now's the time to stop caring. People's sense of humor can vary wildly; find what tickles your funny bone and allow the rest of the world to either laugh with you or be judgmental fuddy-duddies, whichever floats their boat.

• • •

Yield to the power of the Holy Spirit
(prayer)

Dear Lord,
Thank you for the gift of laughter and good humor. Help me to cultivate a lightness of heart in my motherhood that is rooted in knowing and serving you. May I remember that this world is not my home, so that I may not take it as seriously as I take helping to make your kingdom come in my life and in my family. Please give me the grace to love you, my spouse, my children, my neighbors, and myself in times of laughter as well as in times of sorrow.

Come, Holy Spirit—fill me with a good sense of humor.
Amen.

• • •

GPS: God Positioning System
(scripture)

"And Sarah said, 'God has made laughter for me; every one

who hears will laugh over me.'" — Genesis 21:6

"Strength and dignity are her clothing,
and she laughs at the time to come." — Proverbs 31:25

"Then our mouth was filled with laughter,
and our tongue with shouts of joy;
then they said among the nations,
'The LORD has done great things for them.'"
— Psalms 126:2

"He will yet fill your mouth with laughter,
and your lips with shouting." — Job 8:21

"Blessed are you that hunger now, for you shall be satisfied.
Blessed are you that weep now, for you shall laugh."
— Luke 6:21

• • •

Roadside Assistance

(wisdom from the saints and others)

"Serve the Lord with laughter." — Saint Padre Pio

"From silly devotions and sour-faced saints, good Lord,
deliver us." — Saint Teresa of Ávila

"Saints have a sense of humor. … A saint can be defined as
one who has a divine sense of humor, for a saint never takes
this world seriously as the lasting city."
— Venerable Fulton J. Sheen

• • •

Pit Stop

(other resources)

- Help your kids cultivate a sense of humor. Learn to laugh at things (if you don't already) and show them it's okay to enjoy the funny things in life. Share your favorite clean jokes with your children, or look some up joke books online or at the library. My little ones love knock-knock jokes, while my middles like puns, and the teens are intrigued by funny stories.

- Find some good, "clean" comedians. I recommend Tim Hawkins, Jim Gaffigan, Brian Regan, and Kevin James. All of them have clips or shows online to watch for free or rent, and some might have shows available to borrow from your local public library.

- Watch the movie *Moms' Night Out* with a girlfriend or five at your place or theirs. Bonus points if you end the night with really, really bad karaoke!

● ● ●

Your Ideas

_____

_____

_____

_____

_____

• • •

Discuss Amongst Yourselves
(questions)

1. When was the last time you laughed really hard? What was so funny?

2. Are there any roadblocks in your life that might keep you from cultivating a lighter heart? How might you tackle one of those obstacles this week?

3. If you believe God laughs, what in your life is tickling his funny bone these days?

FOR THE LOVE OF GOD, USE YOUR TURN SIGNAL!

((kindness))

"The best way to keep children at home is to make the home atmosphere pleasant, and let the air out of the tires."

— Dorothy Parker

• • •

Once upon a time, when I was about five years old, my mom and I took a walk at a local park. I was passionately arguing with her about Something Very Important. This was, as I recall, a pretty common occurrence when I was growing up. I'm pretty sure I was one of those children grown-ups call "precocious." Anyway, at a certain point in the discussion, Mom stopped walking, took a deep breath, and turned to me.

"Heather," she said, with a big smile, "someday you are going to be a *wonderful* adult!" And then she smiled again.

I smiled back up at her, grabbed her hand in mine, and we continued our walk. I didn't know what was happening with anyone else at the park that day, but my mom thought I was going to be a wonderful adult, and that sounded good to me.

Of course, today, as a seasoned mother of my own very strong-willed children, I see this scenario from a very different, "through the looking glass" perspective. I know that I know that I *know* that my mother was attempting to change the tone and course of our interaction by following what I call the Thumper Protocol. You know Thumper—the bunny from the Disney movie *Bambi*. He got caught saying something unkind, so his mama told him to repeat what she'd undoubtedly spent hours reiterating at home: "If you can't say somethin' nice, don't say nothin' at all."

And that's 100 percent what my mom was doing, I'm sure. I bet Mom was so exasperated that projecting into the future for something kind to say was the best she could do. Yet, rather than losing her cool over how ridiculous I was being and escalating the situation, my mom took the high road by exercising kindness. And by taking that high road, she set us on a path of unity rather than discord.

The golden rule in action

I think, as a young mom, my mother knew the truth that I have since learned myself: "Above all hold unfailing your love for one another, since love covers a multitude of sins" (1 Pt 4:8). She was covering my insolence with a compliment, replacing my undoubtedly harsh words with her loving ones. And what is kindness, if not love in action?

These days we're taught to view tolerance as a virtue, often mistaking it for kindness. Certainly, we are called to, as Saint Paul says, forbear or "put up with" one another, yet we shouldn't mistake tolerance for kindness. I can guarantee that, had my mom's strategy failed to cut off my back talk at the proverbial pass, she wouldn't have hesitated to discipline me. And, trust me, I was disciplined as a kid—*a lot*. By no means are we moms obliged to tolerate wrong behavior from our kiddos. In fact, the kindest thing we can do is to help them learn the right way to behave. But it doesn't hurt to try kindness as a first resort rather than an afterthought.

In my opinion, it isn't possible to take the high road if you're not familiar with a little thing called self-control (more on that in the next chapter). Often, showing kindness is an act of the will. Are we going to take the time to hold the door for the man walking in behind us at the bank? Will we offer up our seat for an elderly woman at Mass? Will we chat with the panhandler at the stoplight, or will we just keep driving? The choice is always ours.

Kindness isn't just "being nice," "being polite," "having good manners," or showing "common courtesy." Kindness has its roots in genuine love for the other. We can fake being nice, polite, well-mannered, or courteous, maybe because we think we stand to gain something, or we don't want to be seen in a negative light, or we feel obliged because of societal norms. Real kindness, on the other hand, sees the image and likeness of God in the other—their dignity, beauty, and inherent worth—and responds with love, whether or not there is something to be gained.

Kindness in our domestic church

Saint Teresa of Calcutta put it so well when she said, "If you want peace in the world, go home and love your family." I believe she said this because sometimes it's harder to show kindness to our family members than "the world." The world doesn't know us deeply and personally. We aren't necessarily vulnerable to the world. The world isn't supposed to love us like our family members are. The world doesn't know as well as our family members how to push our buttons, like leaving the cap off the toothpaste, or fighting nonstop with their brother in the minivan, or leaving the milk out on the table, or bringing home important papers to be signed three days after they're due.

There is no better place to start learning about kindness—love in action—than in our home. There are infinite opportunities to practice kindness, but let's start with the very person reading these words. Jesus told us to love our neighbor (and, for the record, our spouse/children count as "neighbor") as ourselves.

Too often, we busy moms forget the "ourselves" part, not just putting our needs lower on the list than everyone else's, but rather forgetting to put ourselves on the list at all. Sure, there's a culture of self-absorption that believes that "me" time is the end-all, be-all. Left unchecked, "me" time can become an idol—something we spend all our time and energy thinking about and seeking after, believing it will somehow "save" us from our unhappiness and suffering. There's absolutely nothing wrong with solitude, recreation, or kicking back every once in a while. Even God himself rested on the seventh day as an example to us. Granted, we don't want to make an idol out of self-care. We live in God's economy, after all, where to die is to live and to give is to receive. But as we've mentioned before, a mom cannot give what a mom doesn't have. So, let us heed Jesus' words and love—be kind—to ourselves just as fastidiously as we endeavor to be loving and kind to others. Or, as my friend likes to remind me, "Be kind to your kids' mom."

I read a story recently about a family who shared the most time together during meals. It was at the dinner table, according to the mother, that each of her children was able to practice service and kindness, offering food to the person on either side of them before taking something for their own plate, asking if there was anything else they could do for their sibling before they began to eat. With everyone concerned about someone else, each received what he or she needed without having to be selfish about it. Now, the Renshaws haven't exactly implemented this amazing concept in our family, but please check in with me about it. I can just imagine how it would change the tone of mealtime in our home for the better.

In a 2015 general audience, Pope Francis said, "No other school can teach the school of love if the family cannot." This statement both challenges and scares the poop out of me. It sort of throws down the gauntlet for how we are to treat one another within the context of our home. Pope Francis seems to say that if we can't get love right at home, our kids won't get it elsewhere, even in the school of hard knocks. As a mom, I figure I can rise to the challenge, or I can decide it's too hard or too scary and give up.

I pray God I never give up on love. As long as I continue to ask the Holy Spirit to infuse in me the fruit of kindness, especially toward those with whom I live, I can trust that I'm on the right road.

Taking kindness to the streets

What if we decided to extend the borders of our domestic church beyond the confines of our immediate family? We could include that cranky neighbor, the lady with the weird piercings and bumper stickers, the know-it-all colleague, and the homeless guy pushing the two carts down the street.

Ironically, sometimes I find it's easier to be kind to the stranger on the street than it is to be to my own family members. Does that ever happen to you? I mean, the lady at the library who asked me for directions to the bathroom didn't just spit up her peas all over my shirt. And the driver I let in front of me on the highway didn't just spend the last five minutes arguing with me about borrowing my hair dryer. The clerk at the shoe store didn't just hurt my feelings by walking out the door without kissing me goodbye. See what I mean?

Don't get me wrong; strangers can annoy the heck out of us, too (don't believe me? check out social media), but I would submit it's often easier to be on our best behavior—to be kind—when we are in a public setting and there are a lot of witnesses. Nobody wants to be thought of as "that crazy lady" who just arm-wrestled another woman to the ground over the last shopping cart. At least, not in my small town. Word travels fast.

I learned a lot about kindness when we lived in the South. I think my parents did a pretty good job of raising me

to be well-mannered, but the folks down there have elevated
kindness to an art form. (Now, I don't intend to paint everywhere below the Mason-Dixon line with a broad brush, so
bear in mind that these were my impressions and experiences.) First of all, no one was ever in a hurry. There was always
time to chat about the weather, football, and, of course, how
your mama and them (your people, your family) were doing.
Should you have something to discuss that was not of a personal nature, it could wait until you'd exhausted the topics
that stood to build a relationship.

Men still gave up their seats if a place was crowded and a
woman or elderly person needed a place to sit. Hats came off
indoors and during times of prayer. People wouldn't dream
of letting you get the door for yourself. Eye contact was made.
Most places were closed on Sunday, or at least until the afternoon so folks could attend church in the morning.

Every conversation was peppered with "yes, Sir / no,
Sir," "yes, Ma'am / no, Ma'am," "y'all," and "all y'all." It was
also pretty common to be called Sweetie, Baby, Honey, and/
or Sugar by someone taking your order at the drive-through
(which, despite the signs, was never, ever, *fast* food). And, the
funny thing is, I wasn't insulted by strangers addressing me
with such familiar terms of endearment. It just sounded like
someone cared about me enough to get waffle fries and sweet
tea into my hot little hands before I died of heat stroke.

Anyone who has lived in the South has likely faced the
"bless your heart" learning curve. When we first got there,
folks were blessing my heart all over the place, and I thought,
"Wow! What a friendly, friendly place! Everybody is praying
for me!" And, sure enough, many of the "bless your heart"
comments were sincere. About two weeks in, however, I figured out that "bless your heart" could also be the Southern
way of hiding unkind thoughts behind a sweet platitude.

Luckily, I had a friend who corroborated my hunch. "Oh,
yes. If someone thinks you're crazy, or a mess, or whatever,
they'll say, 'Bless your heart,' but you really only have to start
being worried about yourself if they start blessing your 'little,

pea-pickin' heart.' That means they think you're pretty much a lost cause." The more I thought about it, the more I didn't mind all the blessing of my heart. I decided to presume people meant what they said, and I chose to feel they cared. The real truth was between them and God, bless their hearts.

My friend Rebecca shared a story with me about her ninety-two-year-old firecracker of a Southern Catholic grandmother, who, at the time, lived independently and needed some help with a leak in her bathroom. What began as a quick drop-in to fix a drip stretched into a daylong call, and then a two-day job. Although the plumber's incompetence and invasion of her home and schedule was, according to Rebecca's granny, "bugging the crap out of her," she decided to bear her suffering with patience and love, believing it to be better than throat-punching him and kicking him in the knee. When, on the second day, Jimmy (the plumber) told Rebecca's grandmother he wasn't quite done yet, rather than unleashing the power of her laser-like temper, Granny chose to play a hand of kindness instead.

"Jimmy," she told the plumber with a broad smile, "I just want to thank you for being Jesus for me today."

It's possible the plumber thought this nonagenarian had just "blessed his pea-pickin' heart" times one thousand; yet, in fact, Granny was acknowledging that if she bore her inconveniences and irritation with patience and kindness, it could be a highly purifying process for her soul. She truly believed that the plumber was helping her get closer to sainthood. I bet Jimmy just thought Granny was a sweet old lady. Maybe he was having a difficult time at home, and hanging out at Granny's house helped him feel better about life again. We may never know.

Now, some of you may see the examples I've given from living in the South and of my friend's grandmother and say, "That's so fake. Why pretend to be kind when you really want to punch someone?" And I would say: what would you gain by assaulting someone, other than a one-way ride to the local jail? It's true that you might never really know what's in a person's heart, or why they do what they do. You can't judge that. But there are plenty of people who are looking at our actions, wondering whether we are going to love them as we love ourselves like Jesus taught. Scripture tells us that they (defined as people in our homes and beyond) "will know we are Christians by our love." And how will they see our love? Through our acts of kindness.

Everybody needs kindness, but especially …

Since this is my book about motherhood, I can reveal my bias if you haven't guessed already: I think young moms need more kindness than a lot of other populations of people.

Because I know deep, deep down in my knower that the most Pinterest-worthy, Instagram-savvy, soccer/hockey/dance mom who runs her own business and thirteen miles as a warm-up feels like a failure as a mother more often than you and I would ever guess.

Every mom (in fact, every person) is carrying a cross that is painful, heavy, and, more often than not, invisible to the untrained eye. I have learned that just because another mom's cross isn't the same as mine doesn't mean it isn't just as difficult. We are here to help lift one another's burdens, not add to them. One way to help lift the burden is by showing each other intentional kindness.

And truly, what does kindness cost us? Usually, pretty little. Sure, I may not *feel* like making eye contact or smiling or saying hello, but it can be a wonderful thing, both for us and for the person in our midst. As Saint Teresa of Calcutta said, "Every time you smile at someone, it is an action of love, a gift to that person, a beautiful thing." So, do something kind and beautiful for Jesus the next time you don't feel like it: smile.

Recently I've become She Who Smiles at the weary mom herding an energetic crew of children at the grocery store. It's a bit odd since, for so long, *I* was the sweaty, overwhelmed mom struggling to hold it together while cleaning up an infant, toddler, and preschooler on aisle 12.

Now, don't get me wrong—I still get sweaty and over-whelmed—but these days, instead of schlepping diaper bags overflowing with toys, onesies, and stale cereal while sprint-ing after escaping littles, I'm helping our kids schlep the dif-ficult crosses inherent in twenty-first-century childhood and young adulthood. It is still hard; it's just a different varietal of hard. Call it Motherhood: Version 2.0.

Not too long ago, my husband and I went on a dinner date. *Alone.* Gasp! I *know.* Anyway, a young couple dined at the next table over with their passel of progeny. The famil-iar clamor of hungry and energetic tykes angling for tasty morsels and drink cups was being reasonably managed by Dad, while Mom attempted to pacify the newest addition with milk.

As the family finished their meal and began the min-utes-long process of gathering children and belongings, I smiled at the mom and said, "You have a beautiful family."

She sighed and said, "This was our first attempt out to dinner with everyone since the baby was born."

I said, "Well, y'all did great!"

She beamed as she replied, "Thank you! We just might try it again some time."

Last spring, our family packed tightly into a pew at my parents' parish for Easter Sunday Mass. Effusive babbling and constant movement behind me indicated the presence of a busy toddler whose mother was striving to keep him from bothering me. I turned and smiled at Mom and son, assuring her I was just fine, and that she needn't apologize for bring-ing an active little soul to Mass. "What a sweet little guy," I said. "Happy Easter!"

I'm no saint; my husband and children still give me a run for my money every day of the week and twice on Tuesday. I'm just a mom who knows there are other moms (and dads and grandparents and friends and neighbors and strangers) who could likely benefit from a little kindness.

Let's remember that moms all around us—new as well as seasoned—are relentlessly battling difficulties and carrying crosses that you and I may never realize. Presume grace. Share a smile with your immediate family as well as with strangers. And, while you're at it, please be kind to yourself.

• • •

Roadblocks to kindness

Busyness: Sometimes we get so wrapped up in our own lives that we can't see the nose on our neighbor's face. It might be time to slow down, look around, and see who could stand a splash of kindness in their cup. Cookies to a new neighbor, a smile to the gentleman in the back of the church, allowing someone to merge in front of you on the highway—these aren't complicated or expensive things, but if we all added them together, how much kinder would our world be?

Lack of empathy: While I think some people come out of the womb with more innate compassion for their fellow human beings than others, I firmly believe that empathy can be learned by modeling and practicing. Engage in active listening, observe your friend's nonverbal cues while communicating to pick up how she's really doing. Try to anticipate how you can make her day better when she finds out the job interview she just left was a bust.

Weariness: Do you ever just want to stop being kind to everyone and everything and have a "cranky" day and a nap? Maybe that's just me. Parenting is the only job that's 24/7/365. A mama is bound to get tired. Perhaps plotting your next random act of kindness (whether inside or outside your home) will give you just the boost you need to put a smile back on your face.

Negative outlook: Are you an Eeyore by nature or because of current circumstance? Do you say things like, "I don't know why I bother being kind; it's not like it makes a difference anyhow," or "I wish people would just stop being so darn cheerful already." First, check to see if you're actually Old Man Heckles, the cranky neighbor on the popular sitcom *Friends*. Next, think about how being the recipient of someone's kindness has cheered you in the past. Ask the Holy Spirit to help you, little by little through the choices you make, to develop the fruit of kindness, so you can be God's love in action to friends and family.

• • •

Yield to the power of the Holy Spirit

(prayer)

Dear Lord,
I'm so grateful for the kindness you've shown me. Please forgive me for the times when I've failed to recognize this gift. Father, you know that sometimes I'm distracted or irritable and forget to be kind to those with whom I'm closest. Please help me reflect your kindness to my children, my spouse, and myself.

Come Holy Spirit—fill me with your kindness. Amen.

• • •

GPS: God Positioning System

(scripture)

"You shall love your neighbor as yourself." — Mark 12:31

"Do nothing from selfishness or conceit, but in humility count others better than yourselves. Let each of you look not only to his own interests, but also to the interests of others." — Philippians 2:3–4

"Be mindful of your compassion, O LORD, and of your

merciful love,
for they have been from of old."
— Psalms 25:6

"And be kind to one another, tenderhearted, forgiving one another, as God in Christ forgave you." — Ephesians 4:32

• • •

Roadside Assistance

(wisdom from the saints and others)

"If it wasn't for people, we could all be holy."
— Mother Angelica

"Let us always meet each other with a smile, for the smile is the beginning of love." — Saint Teresa of Calcutta

"Don't say: 'That person gets on my nerves.' Think: 'That person sanctifies me.'" — Saint Josemaria Escrivá

"You must not only have a kind word for your neighbors and for strangers, but also for the people with whom you live and your closest friends." — Saint Francis de Sales

• • •

Pit Stop

(other resources)

- Encourage your kids to become Kindness Ninjas, performing various random acts of kindness on a given day for their sibling, a neighbor, or a friend close by. Challenge yourself to do the same.

- Commit to following the Thumper Protocol for one whole day, speaking kindly to and about others and yourself, or not at all. If you can make it one day, challenge yourself to spread it to a whole week!

- My kids and I recommend the live-action version of the movie *Cinderella*, released in 2015. One of the main themes in the movie is, "Have courage, and be kind." See if you can spot any other uplifting or encouraging themes.

● ● ●

Your Ideas

_____

_____

_____

_____

● ● ●

Discuss Amongst Yourselves
(questions)

1. Recall a time when someone showed your family kindness. What was the situation; how did it impact you?

2. Consider a situation where you had the opportunity to respond in kindness, yet didn't. If given the chance, how might you redo your response?

3. Make time to perform one simple "act of kindness" for your family members each day this week. It doesn't need to be fancy, just based on thoughtful consideration of the other person. How do you think this kindness will impact your relationships?

DON'T MAKE ME TURN
THIS CAR AROUND!!

((self-control))

"I always say if you aren't yelling at your kids, you're not spending enough time with them."

— Reese Witherspoon

• • •

I'm sure you'd never sneak the last scoop of ice cream after your kids are in bed. The mere *thought* of yelling at your husband or children, let alone the thoughtless jackwagon who just cut you off in traffic, makes you break out in a cold sweat. And you'd never *dream* of splurging on a household item that isn't on your carefully curated shopping list even if it is super cute *and* on clearance. You, my friend, are a radiant example of self-restraint and refinement, a paragon of graceful parenthood, a model of self-mastery.

And then there's me.

Let's just say I've been waging a heated battle with my archnemesis, self-control, since before I could speak in complete sentences. This struggle makes being a mature, self-sacrificing, other-centric servant of my domestic church downright difficult ... but not impossible, because, well, *God* (see Lk 1:37).

Over the years I've found that I *can* control myself, but usually only in short spurts. Being habitually self-disciplined for the long haul isn't really my thing. I'm naturally impulsive, fly-by-the-seat-of-my-pants, and effusive. These are great traits for getting the dance floor going at a wedding reception or a women's conference, but perhaps not exactly the first qualifications one would seek in a responsible caregiver. Mary Poppins I am not.

Because of my temperament and personality, I know I need to double down on one fruit of the Holy Spirit more than any other: self-control. When I cultivate this fruit properly, it yields an exponential harvest, because it helps me choose to be loving, joyful, peaceful, kind, patient, gentle, good, etc. And I know I need *all* these fruits because, man, it's tough to subjugate my desires for the sake of others all day, every day, come rain or shine.

If you haven't guessed by now, my husband and I are blessed with five, shall we say, *high-spirited* children. My friend Kate calls these sorts of darlings "shiny kids." The Renshaw brand of "shininess" includes amazing creativity, sweet tenderheartedness, and bona fide special needs. It's also peppered with freakish determination, outlandish obstinacy, and a collective volume that would make a death metal convention seem quiet. Here's a prayer I often say: *"Dear Sweet Baby Jesus, please help my children use their powers for good and not for evil. Because you know as well as I that it could go either way. Amen."*

But how will my kids know what to do if I'm not modeling good, godly behavior? I must be the change I want to see in my children—in my family.

Let it all out

It was Thursday. We were getting ready for school as usual when, for whatever reason, everybody developed a severe case of acute amnesia. Suddenly, no one knew what to do to get us out the door on time. Homework was mysteriously missing, uniforms became spontaneously dirty, teeth couldn't get brushed, backpacks were being mauled by the neglected dog, and lunch-making was being flat-out ignored. Despite getting everyone out of bed on time and following the normal morning routine, everything was just "off," and we were running a solid fifteen minutes behind schedule.

Not only were people not doing what they were supposed to do, but they also ignored my helpful instructions for how to get back on track and started turning on each other. Between the debating over whose fault it was that we were late and the arm-wrestling about who would get the last granola bar, I was approaching my capacity for nonsense. I felt my blood pressure rising, and my chest was tighter than an army band drum cadence.

In that moment, I wanted to throttle five-fifths of my children. Instead, I took a few deep breaths, said a Glory Be, and calmly walked away from the bickerpalooza in the kitchen to the relative silence of the garage. I planted my feet firmly on the step facing my minivan (which had exactly zero school-children in it) closed my eyes, and let loose a killer primal yell that vibrated the wall next to me. Once I ran out of air, I took a deep breath and did it again, only louder. Soon enough, kids were running to the garage. "Mom! Are you okay?" "What's going on?" "Are you hurt?" "What WAS that?" they asked. I turned to my beloved offspring and smiled. "Y'all, please get in the van. It's time to go to school," I said, sweet as pie. And, you know what? They *did*. Yes, we were late to school on that particular day, but I'm pretty sure I scared the snot out of them, because we haven't been that late to school since.

Even though I yelled, I considered the experience a "win" in the self-control department. You see, I didn't yell at my *kids*, which is what I really felt like doing in the heat of the moment. It's what I had done way too many times in the past, given similar circumstances. Instead of unleashing my frustration upon my children, I chose to vent my pent-up feelings by yelling at our beleaguered minivan. Mamas, y'all know that our tempers get lost. But if we want to find them again, we need to ask the Holy Spirit for the wisdom to control them and the fortitude to keep them.

Learning to adult

From an early age, parents, teachers, and loved ones try to teach us right from wrong, but darn if our free will doesn't commandeer the wheel and lead us down a dark, twisting road with alarming frequency.

As a child, I wanted to be a grown-up because I thought being a grown-up meant I could do whatever I wanted, whenever I wanted. I actually believed I would be exempt from silly rules, free of lame consequences, and liberated from ridiculous responsibilities. My parents taught me differently, of course; however, like any self-actualized freedom fighter, I chose to ignore them. Boy, was I in for a big and painful wake-up call! During my attempt to launch into "adulthood," I realized my convoluted notion of freedom wasn't exactly sustainable; there were consequences to my actions, just like when I was a kid living under my parents' roof.

My first real job was working for a boutique recruiting firm. One of my responsibilities was driving to various job sites to check in with our clients. I spent a lot of time in my car. (Huh. Sounds familiar.) I'll never forget the day I drove past a local church, a little extra sleepy and not feeling so well from staying out late at a friend's party the night before. On the church's reader board were these words: "To be a disciple, you must have discipline." Now, this happened almost twenty years ago, and I still remember feeling like a huge bomb was going off in my brain. Disciple. *Discipline.* The words were so similar! How had I never seen it before? The root of these two words, I reasoned, must be the same. And, indeed, it is: *discipulus,* which is Latin for pupil, or student. Driving around in my car that day, I realized that, to be a real disciple of Jesus Christ as well as to keep my job, I would have to learn to exercise more discipline over myself and my lifestyle. It was a turning point in my life toward more responsible adulthood.

Now, self-control sounds a whole lot like self-*discipline*, the latter of which I equated with being punished as a kid. Being disciplined meant my parents had grounded me, or a particularly difficult math teacher sent me to the principal's office. (Once! It only happened once!) I mean, really—what sort of person *wants* to be disciplined?

Yet Scripture tells us the Lord disciplines those whom he loves (see Heb 12:4–12). He *teaches* those he loves. He wants us to learn to be more like him. To *love* like him. And we can't be more like Christ if we're off doing whatever we want. And don't we do the same for our children? We discipline them because we want them to learn right from wrong, to develop well-formed consciences. To be joyful, kind, and holy people. And when they're young (and sometimes not-so-young), our kids lack the ability to regulate themselves, so we have to help them. In word *and* in deed.

I firmly believe we need the Holy Spirit to help *us* as well. Because on our own, we will likely smolder, fume, yell, indulge, and drive right off the highway at the first (or ninth) sign of trouble. Or maybe that's just me.

Getting back on the right road

It was only after completely spinning out on the road to hell known as "My Way" that I came to the same conclusion as English historian Lord John Acton, who said, "Liberty is not the power of doing what we *like*, but the right of being able to do what we *ought* (emphasis mine)." When we do only what we want, we actually become enslaved to our lower desires, including overzealous passions, addictions, bad habits, and sinful vices. We aren't actually free at all—just in a bizarre prison of our own design and construction. Trust me: I have the commemorative jailhouse T-shirt that proves this is true.

Saint Paul knew well our tendency toward sin, as he

wrote to the Philippians: "Their end is destruction, their god is the belly, and they glory in their shame, with minds set on earthly things" (3:19).

And it wasn't just "those other people" who were sinning, either. Paul wrote quite a bit about being caught up in doing the sinful things *he* didn't want to do because of his fallen human nature (see Rom 7:15). And, yes, this is *Saint Paul*—who, depending on which version of the Bible you read, wrote around 30 percent of the entire New Testament!

Don't get me started on Saint Augustine, who purportedly asked the Lord to grant him chastity, "just not today." He's a Doctor of the Church. Saint Mary Magdalene, traditionally considered to be the same woman described in the Bible as being possessed by seven demons, was a hot mess before Christ healed her. Her love for the Lord manifested itself in her new role of humble service as the "Apostle to the Apostles." And Saint Thérèse of Lisieux, the Little Flower, struggled with tantrums and fits as a child. She's a Doctor of the Church, too.

If holy men and women—saints and Doctors of the Church!—wrestle with their fallen human natures, maybe that means overworked and underpaid wives and mothers have a chance for sanctification, too. As Saint John Vianney said, "The saints did not all begin well, but they ended well."

But before we level up and storm those Pearly Gates, we must rely heavily on the power of the Holy Spirit to help us control the one person we can possibly control: ourselves.

I can't control the toddler who won't eat her vegetables. Again. Or the kid who accidentally crunches his gaming device when he carelessly leaves it on the floor. Or the baby who, without fail, poops right as we're loading up to leave the house. Heck, Lord knows I can't even control my husband, who—surprise, surprise—is his own person and has free will, too.

The only person I can possibly begin to control is myself, in my thoughts, in my words, and in what I will do, but only with the help of—you guessed it—the Holy Spirit.

We might get cocky at times, thinking we have enough discipline to control ourselves because, after all, we're adults!

We have put away childish things, including wanting our own way. Except ... overtired me wants to hide under the warm comforter on a cold Monday morning and sleep another thirty minutes rather than start the week with quiet prayer before we're off to the races for the day. And feeling-slightly-under-the-weather me doesn't want to "adult" today, either, *thankyouverymuch.* Maybe somebody else can tackle the leaning tower of laundry and ferry children to twenty-seven quadrillion activities and appointments and buy groceries for dinner. Exasperated me wants to drown my sorrows in an overpriced coffee drink when the minivan won't start because a child has, yet again, left the side door open overnight. Overwhelmed me wants to unleash an unholy litany of complaints and frustrations on anyone who will listen.

There are probably things that happen in your household that threaten to send you through the roof, too.

And yet. We don't want to raise whiny, selfish, godless, raging human beings, right? And we definitely don't want to be those sorts of people ourselves. So, we have a decision to make: despite our current workload, emotional state, physical limitations, and perceived injustices, we can choose to practice self-control through the intercession of the Holy Spirit, or we can choose to practice self-indulgence. The fruit of self-control especially doesn't come under our own power. It blossoms the more we put it into practice. It's a result of the Holy Spirit working in our lives.

Remember Jesus words in the Gospel of Mark: "Hear me, all of you, and understand: there is nothing outside a man which by going into him can defile him; but the things which come out of a man are what defile him" (7:14–15). In other words, we must ask the Holy Spirit to help keep us from saying and doing unholy things in response to what happens in our lives, including but not limited to interactions with threenagers, teenagers, and the annoying person we avoid. It's not their fault if we veer off the road; it's ours.

I'm not saying it's going to be easy, my friend. Just ask the overtired, feeling-under-the-weather, exasperated/frustrated/

overwhelmed version of me. I know you've been there, too. But you know that saying, "You can do hard things?" Well, I see your inspirational coffee-mug platitude and raise it one further: we can do *all* things through Christ who strengthens us (see Phil 4:13). Jesus never said that it would be easy to follow him; in fact, he said the opposite (see Jn 16:33). He did say, however, that he would always be with us (see Mt 28:20) and that the Holy Spirit would be with us, too.

When, through the grace of the Spirit, I engage my free will to be more loving, joyful, peaceful, kind, good, gentle, and the rest even when I don't *feel* like it, I'm on track to building God's kingdom here on earth. Catholic author Matthew Kelly might say I'm becoming the best version of myself.

I'd just say that my children have a holier navigator to look up to.

• • •

Here are some signposts for practicing self-control

- Self-control gets us to Mass on Sunday even when we've stayed out too late the night before or are on vacation.

- Self-control keeps us out of the drive-through line when we have food at home but just don't feel like cooking.

- Self-control helps us get some chores done before scrolling through social media. It also helps us be truly present with our children when we'd rather be doing [*fill-in-the-activity*].

- Self-control keeps us from hitting the snooze button so we can have quiet time with the Lord instead.

- Self-control keeps us from overcommitting to too many activities for ourselves and our children.

- Self-control helps us choose love when we're angry, peace when we're upset, gentleness when we're agitated, and kindness when we're tired.

- What does self-control help *you* do?

• • •

Yield to the power of the Holy Spirit
(prayer)

Dear Lord,
You know that we live in a culture that glorifies self-gratification and pleasure. Sometimes, like Saint Paul, I am weak and do the things I do not want to do. I have a difficult time controlling my thoughts, my feelings, my words, and my actions. Please send your Holy Spirit to cultivate the fruit of self-control in my life, so that I may deny myself, take up my cross, and follow you as your faithful disciple. May I, by the help of your grace, become a virtuous and godly example for my family and neighbors alike.

Come, Holy Spirit—fill me with your self-control. Amen.

• • •

GPS: God Positioning System
(scripture)

"A man without self-control
is like a city broken into and left without walls."
— Proverbs 25:28

"I can do all things in him who strengthens me."
— Philippians 4:13

"We destroy arguments and every proud obstacle to the

knowledge of God, and take every thought captive to obey
Christ." — 2 Corinthians 10:5

"For God did not give us a spirit of timidity but a spirit of
power and love and self-control." — 2 Timothy 1:7

"Know this, my beloved brethren. Let every man be quick
to hear, slow to speak, slow to anger, for the anger of man
does not work the righteousness of God." — James 1:19–20

"And he said to all, 'If any man would come after me, let
him deny himself and take up his cross daily and follow
me.'" — Luke 9:23

• • •

Roadside Assistance

(wisdom from the saints and others)

"The devil once declared that if he could have the first moment of the day, he was sure of all the rest."
— Saint John Vianney

"They who, by a generous effort, make up their minds to
obey, acquire great merit; for obedience by its sacrifices
resembles martyrdom." — Saint Ignatius of Loyola

"Good example is the most efficacious apostolate. You must
be as lighted lanterns and shine like brilliant chandeliers
among men. By your good example and your words, ani-
mate others to know and love God."
— Saint Mary Joseph Rossello

"Renounce yourself in order to follow Christ; discipline
your body; do not pamper yourself, but love fasting."
— Saint Benedict

"With that slowness, with that passivity, with that reluctance to obey, what damage you do to the apostolate and what satisfaction you give to the devil."
— Saint Josemaría Escrivá

"A man who governs his passions is master of his world. We must either command them or be enslaved by them. It is better to be a hammer than an anvil."
— Saint Dominic de Guzman

"Rise up then in the morning with the purpose that (please God) the day shall not pass without its self-denial, with a self-denial in innocent pleasures and tastes, if none occurs to mortify sin. Let your very rising from your bed be a self-denial; let your meals be self-denials. Determine to yield to others in things indifferent, to go out of your way in small matters, to inconvenience yourself (so that no direct duty suffers by it), rather than you should not meet with your daily discipline."
— Saint John Henry Newman

• • •

Pit Stop

(other resources)

- Find an inspirational quote or passage about self-control, discipline, or discipleship that speaks to you, and pin it up where you'll see it.

- When I was a kid, my mom had the opportunity to hear Dr. Maya Angelou speak at a national teachers' conference. One of the many quotes I remember mom sharing was this: "If you don't like something, change it. If you can't change it, change your attitude." In other words, we are in charge of our own behavior, our own attitude toward life. As the Rev. Charles Swindoll famously said,

"Life is 10 percent what happens to us and 90 percent how we respond to it."

- Now, Mom never heard this inspirational figure speak, but I like it anyway:

"Educate your children to self-control, to the habit of holding passion and prejudice and evil tendencies subject to an upright and reasoning will, and you have done much to abolish misery from their future and crimes from society." — Benjamin Franklin

• • •

Your Ideas

_____

_____

_____

_____

_____

_____

_____

_____

• • •

Discuss Amongst Yourselves

(questions)

1. Is exercising self-control generally easy or difficult for you? Why do you think this is?

2. Consider a situation when you were self-disciplined. What was the situation, and how did it benefit you and/ or others?

3. What are your biggest roadblocks to exercising self-control? What are two or three things you can do this week to get back on course?

4. How would your life and the lives of your loved ones improve if you faithfully cultivated this fruit in your life?

U-TURNS ENCOURAGED

((forgiveness))

*"He heals the brokenhearted,
and binds up their wounds."*

— *Psalms 147:3*

• • •

I t all began with a rock.

When we arrived in the conference room, the other women and I were each instructed to pick up a rock from the small pile on the floor and take a seat. Next, our retreat master asked us to sit quietly with eyes closed, rocks on our laps, as we listened to his reflection. I closed my eyes, breathed deeply, and considered his words, measured and gentle, against the dull hum of the box fan pushing the warm air around the room on this unseasonably warm fall day.

The woman was utterly desperate, Father Peter said, in agonizing physical pain from more than a dozen years of hemorrhaging every single day. She spent every last cent she had seeking some remedy, some relief, some resolution. And yet, despite consulting with various physicians and attempting untold medicines and practices, she continued to bleed. And because of her affliction, as per cultural Jewish determination, the woman was cursed: unclean, unworthy, and shunned. Her physical pain was compounded because of the wholesale rejection by her people. She had become a shadow of her former self. Somehow, though, the woman had heard about this *Yeshua*—this teacher—a rabbi with a reputation for speaking with authority and bringing healing to those in need. *"If only I touch the hem of his garment,"* she thought to herself, *"I will be healed."*

Once Father completed his reflection, we opened our eyes, and he explained the exercise: "I want you to look at your rock and think about what it represents. Really think about it. What have you been holding on to? What issue or situation is keeping you from allowing Christ to heal you? What do you need to release to Jesus?" He paused, then continued. "We'll go around the room and share what our rock represents for each of us, and then I want you to take your rock and place it at the foot of the cross. You're going to give it to Jesus to keep."

Wait. What? Share? As in, *out loud?* Suddenly, my mind was racing. Did I misunderstand the instructions? *Oh crap,* I thought, as the first woman began to speak. *Nope—she's definitely talking. Wait just one darn minute,* I fumed. *This is not what I signed up for*!

I *thought* I signed up for a silent retreat at the same retreat house where I'd spent pockets of fruitful time in prayerful reflection in the past. In silence. As in, *quiet.* No talking, no conversations, and *definitely* no sharing. Only Jesus, praying, reading, eating, and sleeping were allowed. Period. Where I had been completely freaked out on my first silent retreat because I couldn't interact with the other attendees, this time around I was super annoyed that I was being asked to share! Oy. What a difference a few years makes.

Anyone who knows me for longer than five minutes

knows that I enjoy talking about as much as other people enjoy breathing. I likely have been talking since before the dawn of time. I'm neither shy nor reserved; in fact, I have never met a microphone I didn't love, and I'll tell you all about it. While speaking directly into the microphone. And yet, here I was, in all my extroverted glory, gripped by mind-numbing fear. I'd signed up for this retreat to check out, hole up, and hang on to Jesus for dear life. Alone. In silence. *Please don't make me talk*, I silently shouted in Father Peter's direction. I was afraid of what might come out of my mouth.

I'd come to this retreat during a period of intense pain and frustration. Relationships at home were strained: finances were perpetually tight, and the never-ending demands of work outside the home and the needs of a growing young family life were sucking my will to live. There were other challenges, too—major issues that could, if left unchecked, deal death blows to our marriage, ripping our family apart.

Despite a desire to heal and strengthen our family, my husband and I had been growing increasingly distant from each other. The children sensed the strain and began acting out at home and at school. I felt like a complete and utter failure as a wife and mother—a failure as a human being. What sort of woman, I wondered, thinks she can minister to others when her own family is hanging together by a thread? *A stupid, ridiculous, hypocritical one,* came the accusatory response.

In an attempt to revive my spirit, I was really looking forward to a rare weekend alone, immersed in that rarest of commodities in a busy mother's life: blessed, dedicated silence. Once the noise inside my shell-shocked brain finally died down, I prayed I would find rest and, hope against hope, healing.

But now I was here, in the dreaded Sharing Circle of Death. *What if I just get up and leave?* I thought. But some unknown force made me stay in my seat.

Woman after woman identified her rock, briefly explaining what it was that she wanted to lay at the foot of the makeshift altar Father had erected, complete with a small crucifix standing guard above. "I'm afraid my illness will return," said one woman. "My son is far away from God," lamented another. "I know I need to go to confession, but I'm afraid," shared a third. One by one, these women bared their souls, then stood up and laid their rocks—their most intimate burdens—at the foot of the cross.

The other women's voices gradually faded into the background as I was consumed with my own thoughts. It wasn't that I didn't care about these other women—I truly did—but I grew increasingly agitated by the swirling of my own insecurities: *Why am I here? Why am I holding this stupid rock? Father said I'm supposed to figure out what it represents? I don't know! How about "d."—all of the above?*

And then a still, small voice cut through my internal babbling: "*My daughter, I have brought you to this place. Do not be afraid.*"

Shifting slightly in the vinyl dining room chair upon which I sat, I took a very deep breath. Like a petulant preschooler being redirected by her teacher, I grudgingly looked back down at my rock, moving it from one hand to the other. As I inspected its gray, weighted form, I noted a thin yet pronounced crack that ran its length, spanning the gradual bumps and shallow ridges. Bit by bit, I began to see the rock with new eyes, and I was amazed to realize that it resembled a heart—not the kind you see on romantic greeting cards, but an anatomically correct human heart. It had been years since I'd taken a course on anatomy and physiology, but the longer I looked, the more I realized the stark truth staring me dead in the face: this rock was not just any heart. It was *my* heart. And it had grown increasingly hard, cold, and on the verge of breaking. I knew the unmatched pain of heartbreak; I'd been down that road before. But the particular wound I carried within me to the retreat house that day was heavier and deeper than any I'd previously encountered. And I just couldn't let it go.

For months now, perhaps years, I'd been choosing to

withhold genuine forgiveness and reconciliation in an effort to protect myself from the pain that relentlessly buffeted the sides of my raggedy, battle-weary life raft. I'd constructed a patchwork of armor around my heart so that when disappointment, frustration, sorrow, and anger threatened, I'd be protected, avoiding pain and preserving my sense of self. Only, I realized, that's not how it worked. Maybe I'd kept some of the bad things out, but I'd also inadvertently closed myself off to the One who desired nothing less than to completely heal me from within. Consequently, I progressively became even more wounded than I was before. While I feverishly worked to keep All The Bad Things out, yet blocked All The Good Things from coming in. And I knew the poison of unforgiveness was, slowly but surely, killing me.

In the quiet calm of the conference room, the reality of why I'd been brought to this moment in time began to sink in, one hot tear at a time. The first rolled down my cheek. And then the second. And then more. Until the tears were silently streaming, and I couldn't see my rock anymore.

I was the woman with the hemorrhage. *I* needed the healing touch of Jesus to save me before my flow of bitterness, anger, and self-pity eventually destroyed me. I needed to choose to forgive.

We're only as sick as our secrets

Consumed with this revelation, I was suddenly aware of the silence around me and looked up, realizing it was my turn to speak. "And what does your rock represent, Heather?" Father prompted, gently.

I wiped my eyes with the back of my hand and looked back at my rock. I slowly breathed in and out to steady myself prior to responding. *"Be not afraid,"* the voice reassured.

"Well, Father," I quietly began. "My rock represents my heart." I stopped for a quick moment to catch my breath, and haltingly continued. "And my heart has grown very hard— just like this rock, in fact—because I have been trying to protect it from being hurt." And then I said: "My husband and

I are really struggling, and have been, it seems, forever. I am hurting and feel alone most days. I feel like a complete failure as a mom, like I'm just messing up with my children left and right. And on my rock, you can see," I pointed to the crevice, "there's this line where it's just about ready to crack." Tears fell again like warm rain as I continued. "I have been trying everything I can to make the pain go away. It's really why I came for the retreat this weekend. I kept thinking that," and now the tears were really flowing, and it was difficult to get the words out, "if only I could touch the hem of his garment, maybe this pain I've been carrying would finally go away."

I stopped for a moment, getting ready to stand up and carry my rock over to the pile with the others. But before I could move, Father gently queried, "And what do you think God wants to do with your heart?" I wiped my eyes again, breathed out, and said, realizing the truth as the words tumbled out: "God wants me to soften my heart so he can come in and heal me. He wants me to forgive those who have hurt me. He wants me to forgive myself."

What happened next still gives me goose bumps just thinking about it. Father took something that looked like a handmade blanket of sorts and held it aloft. "This is a *tallit*, a Jewish prayer shawl," he explained. "Teachers—rabbis—at the time of Christ would wear these. When the woman with the hemorrhage reached to touch the hem of Jesus' garment, she was likely grasping for one of these tassels." He placed the shawl across his shoulders. "It looked something like this."

You could hear a collective gasp in the room, but I was most aware of my own response. The message I heard mere minutes earlier, *"My daughter, I have brought you here,"* echoed in my ears.

We were invited to, one by one, come forward and touch the *tallit*, to take its tassels in our hands, feel the threads between our fingers, and, like the woman with the hemorrhage, believe that Jesus could make us whole.

When it was my turn, I could barely see the garment through my waterfall of tears. My hands felt their way to a small textured ball of yarn finished with soft fringe, and I grasped one in my right hand, then another in my left. *"I believe you can heal my heart, Lord,"* I whispered.

And in that moment, time stood still. My heart broke in the most mysterious and beautiful way possible—the way through which the Holy Spirit himself enters into the cracks and administers the divine dose of merciful grace to bring healing and wholeness to a weary soul. *Your faith, daughter, has healed you.*

In that moment, I was keenly aware that, like the woman with the hemorrhage, my journey to wholeness had resumed thanks to the intervention of a teacher named Jesus Christ.

● ● ●

Roadblocks to forgiveness

Many of us carry the burden of unforgiveness around with us. It weighs us down, slows us up, and keeps us from being fully alive in the peace, joy, and love Christ desires for us.

My dear friend, to whom in your past or present do you need to extend forgiveness? What is keeping you from bringing this hurt to the Lord for help and healing? He wants nothing more than for you to be made whole. He came, as we learn in the Gospel of John, for you to have life in abundance (see Jn 10:10)! Do you truly believe this? Will you trust him with your heart? Will you choose to forgive those who have hurt you? Will you choose to forgive yourself?

Here are some common roadblocks that keep us from offering forgiveness:

Fear: Perhaps we're afraid to forgive because we think it will only open us up to being hurt yet again. Unfortunately, there are no guarantees that you'll never be hurt once you forgive; however, until you choose to forgive, there will always be a festering wound eating away at you from the inside. So long as we remain bound by unforgiveness, the hurt remains without an opportunity to genuinely and completely heal.

Justice: We don't want to forgive because we think that, by doing so, we are saying what the other person did was okay. Maybe we want to be sure the offending party is punished. Forgiveness doesn't mean you forget what happened, and it doesn't let the other person off the hook. As Christians, we are called to love our enemies, do good to those who hate us, bless those who curse us, and pray for those who abuse us (see Lk 6:27-36). Forgiving the other person puts you in right order with God and neighbor.

Sadness/Anger/Hurt: It could be that we just are too upset by what happened to want to forgive. In times like these, we must ask the Holy Spirit for the strength to choose to forgive, despite our feelings. Employing your free will to offer mercy when you've been wronged is a powerful witness to and testimony of God's love.

No desire to reconcile: Forgiveness is not the same as reconciliation. Choosing to forgive someone is something you can do on your own, while reconciliation requires both parties. Sometimes reconciliation isn't possible—or even desirable. In fact, in the Bible, we see that Paul and Barnabas, both zealous for the Lord, decided to go their separate ways after a serious conflict. While we should do whatever we can to be at peace with others, sometimes it's best to forgive, shake the dust from our feet, and move on. Indeed, God isn't asking us to forge or continue highly toxic and unsafe relationships.

Sometimes the very first step to unlocking the chains that hold us captive begins with this simple prayer: "Lord, I desire to *want* to forgive. Please help me."

I hope that you will encounter Christ's transforming mercy—realizing that, even in your brokenness, no matter what hurts you may have, you can be made beautifully whole through the outpouring of the unfathomable and lavish love of the Holy Spirit.

• • •

Yield to the power of the Holy Spirit

(prayer)

Dear Heavenly Father,
You know my wounds; you have counted all my tears. Lord, I no longer wish to be held captive by the chains of resentment, animosity, regret, shame, guilt, and unforgiveness. I am ready to leave my burdens at the foot of the cross and be free. Please send your Holy Spirit to help me lay my burdens down and to forgive all those who have hurt me.

Come, Holy Spirit—fill me with your divine mercy and forgiveness. Amen.

• • •

GPS: God Positioning System

(scripture)

"And Jesus said, 'Father, forgive them; for they know not what they do.'" — Luke 23:34

"And forgive us our trespasses,
As we forgive those who trespass against us."
— Matthew 6:12

"A new heart I will give you, and a new spirit I will put within you; and I will take out of your flesh the heart of stone and give you a heart of flesh." — Ezekiel 36:26

"For if you forgive men their trespasses, your heavenly Father also will forgive you;
but if you do not forgive men their trespasses, neither will your Father forgive your trespasses." — Matthew 6:14–15

• • •

Roadside Assistance
(wisdom of the saints and others)

"To withhold forgiveness is to take poison and expect the unforgiven to die." — Saint Augustine

"Nothing so likens you to God, as to forgive him who has injured you." — Saint Thomas Aquinas

"Forgiveness is above all a personal choice, a decision of the heart to go against the natural instinct to pay back evil with evil." — Pope Saint John Paul II

"The Lord has loved me so much: we must love everyone … we must be compassionate!" — Saint Josephine Bakhita

"No one heals himself by wounding another."
— Saint Ambrose

• • •

Pit Stop
(other resources)

- Experience the freedom that comes from making a good confession. Check out www.masstimes.org for confession times near you.

- Read *Beautiful Mercy* or *Everybody Needs to Forgive Somebody*, both available via Dynamic Catholic.

- Pray the Divine Mercy Chaplet. If you're unfamiliar with this powerful devotion prayed using ordinary rosary beads, visit https://www.marian.org/whatwedo/divine-mercy.php for more information.

- Seek counsel with a trusted friend, spiritual adviser, priest, religious, or licensed therapist for help moving on from hurt and unforgiveness.

● ● ●

Your Ideas

_____

_____

_____

_____

_____

_____

● ● ●

Discuss Amongst Yourselves
(questions)

1. Consider a time in your life when it was difficult to forgive. What prevented you from extending mercy? How were you able to finally lay your burden at the foot of the cross?

2. Talk about a time you received someone's forgiveness and mercy in your life. What impact did it have?

3. Think about the one person you need to forgive; perhaps it is yourself. What steps will you take toward healing this week?

THANK GOD, WE MADE IT!

((gratitude))

"Gratitude ... turns what we have into enough, and more. It turns denial into acceptance, chaos into order, confusion into clarity ... makes sense of our past, brings peace for today, and creates a vision for tomorrow."

— *Melody Beattie*

• • •

We were finally moving back to my beloved Oregon. Even though we could see God's fingerprints all over the circumstances that made our return possible, it was bittersweet to leave dear friends and a wonderful new community behind. We were determined, however, to put our trust in the Lord, confident we were obeying his will.

The cross-country move from Alabama back to the Pacific Northwest, sadly, was anything but smooth sailing. In hindsight, I believe it took several actual miracles and a fleet of overworked guardian angels to get our family back to Oregon in one piece. Things were off to a rocky start when I realized my husband had booked two hotel rooms for our family of seven, which meant he and I would be sleeping separately. I mean, it made sense logistically, but after driving long days in different vehicles to the hotel *du jour*, I was looking forward to the one familiar comfort of falling asleep with David by my side. He promised he had told me about the arrangements before we left Alabama. I promised him, rather loudly, that he most certainly had *not*.

After our first day on the road, one of our vehicles (I won't say which) ran out of gas about half a mile from our hotel. This meant that one of us (I won't say who) had to drive through unfamiliar territory in the dark to track down a service station to fill a gas can and return to the aforementioned vehicle while hungry children bemoaned the postponement of their final meal of the day like a pack of rabid wolves.

The next day, after another marathon driving session, we decided to take advantage of the hotel pool before hitting the sack. We figured it might help the kids tolerate our grueling travel schedule better if they had a little fun. It seemed like a wonderful idea until I noticed our eldest son drifting from the shallow end to the deep end of the pool where he could no longer touch bottom. His head bobbing and arms climbing, I panicked as my boy quickly became a poster child for silent drowning. "GRAB NOAH NOW!!!" I screamed at my husband and, in no time flat, Noah was wrapped tightly within my arms on the safe, concrete pool deck. I've never in my life been so grateful for my husband's long limbs and catlike reflexes. Pool time was over.

The next morning, our toddler disappeared into the hotel hallway while we were packing up to leave. Apparently, the last person in the room the night before failed to lock the deadbolt, and Kolbe knew how to open the door leading into the hotel corridor after all. That child could grow up to be a ninja or a spy, because no one noticed the door open or saw him leave. At some point, I heard crying in the hallway, which made me pause from my task to look up, thinking how there was another toddler staying on the same floor as us, which made me look for my toddler, which made me realize he was missing. "WHERE'S KOLBE??!!!" I screamed. After looking under beds and in closets, we raced into the hallway, only to find him being consoled in the arms of a compassionate stranger. "Did you lose a baby?" she asked as I sprinted toward my child. I grabbed Kolbe in my arms and nearly dropped dead right there. I thanked the kind lady, rushed my son and the other children into the room with my husband, and locked myself in the bathroom for about fifteen minutes while I sobbed.

The next night, as we neared our stopping point outside Denver, a deer the size of Bambi's dad bolted onto the road out of nowhere and almost took out not one but both of our vehicles. I had to stop driving for a little while after that incident; I was shaking too much.

And then, somewhere on a Utah highway, tire rubber started flying at my windshield. I soon realized it was coming from the trailer my husband was pulling just ahead of me. Luckily, we were near an exit, and the minivan pulled the gimpy trailer to a safe place near a truck stop. Three anxious hours later, we finally had a new tire on the trailer and were back on the road, hoping to make up time so we wouldn't derail our tight driving schedule.

On the second-to-last day of our trip, I was ready to collapse from exhaustion and stress. If I had to endure one more crisis or one more stop on the side of the road for a preschooler who said she had to go potty but actually had no intention of doing anything of the sort, I was going to spontaneously combust.

I can think of very few times in adulthood when I've been grasping at the unraveling ends of my proverbial rope as desperately as during our move back to Oregon. The infamous story about Saint Teresa of Ávila crossed my mind: as she was returning to her convent during a rainstorm, the wheel of her carriage broke, and Saint Teresa was thrown into the mud. She reportedly yelled to the heavens, "If this is how you treat your friends, no wonder you have so few!"

I could relate.

Here we were, trying to obey God, following his will, and we were met with turmoil and strife at every turn. It was, to say the least, quite disheartening.

As we began our second-to-last travel day, I honestly didn't know how I was going to continue for another minute, let alone another forty-eight hours. I silently prayed for God to take this cup away from me. Suddenly, I felt a nudge to play some music. I know that it wasn't my idea, because I had a splitting tension headache, and listening to music was close to the last thing on my mind. And yet, I asked my eldest daughter to look in the glove box for a CD. Sure enough, there was a disc of contemporary Gospel music sitting right on top, collecting dust. I have no idea how long it had been there, but something told me we were supposed to play it.

The first song was a mid-tempo jam featuring a sturdy bass line, with the singer relating all God has done by dying, rising, and saving us. The second was an up-tempo crowd-pleaser proclaiming how good God is all the time, with an emphasis on "all." The third was a song I'd sung several years before as part of the Oregon Symphony's Gospel Christmas concerts, about how God is with us no matter what. I sang along at the top of my lungs, much to my children's consternation.

By the time we got to the fourth song, a contemporary take on the old hymn "'Tis So Sweet," I laughed as I sang about trusting in Jesus, taking him at his word, and resting on his promise. I just knew that this—offering a sacrifice of praise and gratitude even in the midst of our relentless storm—was exactly what I should have been doing all along.

It wasn't long before I was thanking God out loud as I drove, and I encouraged my kids to do the same. We thanked him for his great provision, allowing us to relocate closer to family members. We thanked him for covering us with his blood, for sending his angels to protect us from drowning, kidnapping, deer, and car wrecks. We thanked him for fruit snacks and clean toilets at the rest stop. Less than half an hour before, I had been ready to throw in the towel and abandon hope of ever reaching our destination. Now, the Holy Spirit kept my internal motor rolling with praise and worship music.

Deciding to be grateful

Not every week is going to be as tumultuous and traumatic as the one we spent driving across the country in our minivan, but it's tempting to give in to resentment, self-pity, and discouragement when times are tough. When I choose to be indifferent or ignore my many blessings, what kind of a life am I leading, and what kind of example am I providing for my children? I would much rather find a reason to praise and thank God than to be a miserable wretch with dry, lifeless bones.

Thankfully, being dismal and comatose is not what God wants for any of his beloved children. I believe the Holy Spirit animates our ability to praise and thank God, even in difficult moments, but we have to make the choice to do so.

I remember an example from *The Hiding Place*, a book by Holocaust survivor Corrie ten Boom. She said that the bedbugs were so bad in their barracks that the soldiers, who would regularly overwork and beat the women in the camp, left them alone. So they thanked God for the bedbugs.

If someone in a concentration camp can thank God for bugs, I think I can work on thanking God for the dirty dishes, because it means we had food to eat. The massive piles of unfolded laundry means we have clothing to wear. The constantly dirty floors to sweep (and mop, oh gosh, I need to mop) mean we have a place to live. Come to think of it, pretty much anything I can complain about has a flip side for which I can be grateful. Like Saint Teresa of Calcutta said, "Wash the plate not because it is dirty nor because you are told to wash it, but because you love the person who will use it next." I would add: wash the plate because you are grateful for the plate, the food that filled it, the people who ate from it, and the running water with which to wash it clean again.

What would my life look like if I leaned into my vocation with so much gratitude that I fell on my knees in thanksgiving for all of God's gifts and blessings? It would probably be much less painful than wallowing in the muck and mire of self-pity and negativity.

Does a positive mindset mean all the hard, uncomfortable, painful things in life magically disappear? I wish; but no, it doesn't. We will always have trials and suffering; it's the nature of our human existence. But we can choose to make the effort to remember God's goodness and provision, even during those events and circumstances that don't look or feel like gifts in the moment.

One of my go-to mama mantras is, "Everything is grace." Car won't start? Well, that's actually grace. Unexpected money in our mailbox? That's grace, too. A sick kid changes my plans? Yep, you guessed it—grace. All of it. Every last bit. And while I wish I could take credit for the concept, it actually comes from the book *Story of a Soul* by Saint Thérèse of Lisieux. The full text: "Everything is a grace, everything is the direct effect of our Father's love—difficulties, contradictions, humiliations, all the soul's miseries, her burdens, her needs—everything, because through them she learns humility, realizes her weakness. Everything is a grace because everything is God's gift."

I pray the Holy Spirit gives us the grace to live in this Eucharistic reality—a life of constant gratitude and thanksgiving. As the old blessing before meals says, "For what we are about to receive, may the Lord make us truly thankful." No matter what. Amen!

● ● ●

Roadblocks to gratitude

Complacency: I don't know about you, but I sure can take my blessings for granted. I don't always think to thank God for my minivan, my appliances, or my health … until something breaks down. Let's ask the Holy Spirit to help us to not overlook any of the many gifts he has given us.

Sense of entitlement: Oh, this is one of my biggest pet peeves. When I observe people (especially in my immediate family) acting like something is owed them as opposed to a sheer blessing from the Lord for which they should be thankful, I want to run screaming into the hills. Hopefully, with God's help, we can learn to recognize how incredibly fortunate we are, and not assume that we deserve any of it.

Too many things: It can be difficult to thank God when we don't even remember what we have. It's not uncommon for many families to have an overabundance of, well, stuff. Rather than keeping things we don't need or use, perhaps it's time to pare down and donate items in good condition so they can be a blessing to those in need. (Note to self. Ha, ha!)

• • •

Yield to the power of the Holy Spirit

(prayer)

Dear Jesus,
I praise and thank you, for you are my Lord and my God.
Thank you so much for all your many blessings—the gift of my life, my faith, my vocation to marriage and to motherhood. Please help me to be grateful for those blessings I recognize as gifts as well as those that are yet to be revealed.

Come, Holy Spirit—fill me with abiding gratitude. Amen.

• • •

GPS: God Positioning System

(scripture)

"O give thanks to the LORD, for he is good;
for his mercy endures forever!"
— 1 Chronicles 16:34

"The LORD is my strength and my shield; in him my heart
trusts;
so I am helped, and my heart exults, and with my song I
give thanks to him." — Psalms 28:7

"And let the peace of Christ rule in your hearts, to which
indeed you were called in the one body. And be thankful.
Let the word of Christ dwell in you richly, as you teach
and admonish one another in all wisdom, and as you sing
psalms and hymns and spiritual songs with thankfulness in
your hearts to God. And whatever you do, in word or deed,
do everything in the name of the Lord Jesus, giving thanks
to God the Father through him." — Colossians 3:15–17

"Have no anxiety about anything, but in everything by
prayer and supplication with thanksgiving let your requests
be made known to God." — Philippians 4:6

"Enter his gates with thanksgiving, and his courts with praise!
Give thanks to him, bless his name!" — Psalms 100:4

"You have turned my mourning into dancing; you have
loosed my sackcloth
and clothed me with gladness,
that my soul may praise you and not be silent. O LORD my
God, I will give thanks to you forever." — Psalms 30:11–12

"And you will say in that day:
'Give thanks to the LORD,
call upon his name;
make known his deeds among the nations,
proclaim that his name is exalted.
Sing praises to the LORD, for he has done gloriously;
let this be known in all the earth.'" — Isaiah 12:4–5

● ● ●

Roadside Assistance

(wisdom from the saints)

"O my God, let me remember with gratitude, and confess to thee thy mercies toward me." — Saint Augustine of Hippo

"In all created things discern the providence and wisdom of God, and in all things give him thanks."
— Saint Teresa of Ávila

"Prayer is an aspiration of the heart, it is a simple glance directed to heaven, it is a cry of gratitude and love in the midst of trial as well as joy." — Saint Thérèse of Lisieux

"Thank God ahead of time." — Blessed Solanus Casey

● ● ●

Pit Stop

(other resources)

Gratitude Rosary: My friend Lauren posted recently about offering prayers of thanksgiving with a Rosary. As you pray the Rosary, name something or someone for whom you are thankful. On each bead take a moment to meditate on the gratitude you have for the person/place/moment and how it has blessed your life or brought you closer to Christ.

Gratitude journal: When my friend Rebecca was going through an extremely difficult time, she began writing down five things for which she was grateful every night. She says it forced her to look during the day for blessings instead of challenges. At first, she wrote down simple things like, "I woke up today," and "I was able to tie my shoes." Eventually, she even began seeing the challenges as blessings. She said reframing her circumstances through the lens of gratitude made a huge impact in her life.

You could start a journal just for giving thanks to God, too. Start small, listing a few things each day for which you are grateful, or write letters to God expressing your thanks for his many blessings. (Tip: your journal may be simple or fancy, but make sure it fits in your purse, diaper bag, or glove box so you can take it with you on the road.)

Gratitude attitude check: Several children back, I purchased a small sign that reads, "All because two people fell in love." I hung it where I'd see it, right above where the kids usually made the biggest messes in the family room. The sign reminded me that love unleashed an avalanche of kid chaos into my life, and I should never take that love—or those kids—for granted. It's been a good thought to keep in mind when I'm corralling toys for the 996,000th time. Do you have some visible sign in your home that reminds you to be grateful for your blessings?

Gratitude chores: I'm not a huge fan of domestic chores in general, but laundry in particular makes me twitch. To offset some of this internal angst, I began praying for my husband as I was hanging his work shirts to dry. As I buttoned, I thanked God for the gift he is to me, for the blessing of his job (which is why he wears the shirts in the first place), for his health, and for other intentions. I try to pray in thanksgiving for various things whenever I do dishes, or sweep, or whatever, especially for my children when they're being particularly, um, *shiny*. It improves my outlook, and I think it gives glory to God, too.

Other ideas: Send a text, email, or (bonus!) a snail-mail card to someone for whom you're thankful. Tell them why they're amazing!

Spend a holy hour (or just ten minutes!) in adoration. Dedicate your time to thanking God for his many blessings.

Look up Mary's Magnificat prayer, found in Luke 1:46–55. Meditate on Mary's gratitude to God and ask the Holy Spirit to fill your heart with similar thanksgiving. Write out the prayer, or even pray it aloud as a form of worship to God.

• • •

Your Ideas

_____

_____

_____

_____

_____

• • •

Discuss Amongst Yourselves
(questions)

1. Think of a time when something was really difficult yet eventually became a blessing. What happened, and were you eventually able to thank and praise God for it?

2. Do you make praise and thanksgiving a regular part of your prayer time? If so, perhaps change things up and express your gratitude in a new way this week. If not, consider dedicating more time to thankfulness while praying, starting today.

3. List some practical ways you can continue or begin cultivating a life of gratitude this week.

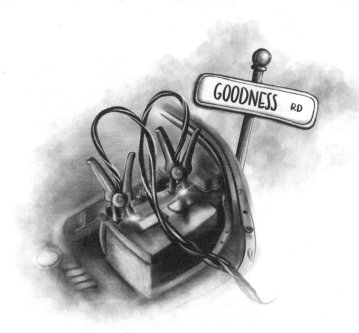

IT'S WHAT'S UNDER THE HOOD THAT COUNTS

((goodness))

"Don't be so hard on yourself. The mom in E.T. the Extraterrestrial had an alien living in her house for days and didn't notice."

— Unknown

● ● ●

Everything I ever needed to know about how self-centered and wounded I am, I learned after I'd been married for a couple of years. The honeymoon period, where everything is fresh and new and exciting, eventually fades, and then you're doing the real work of your sacrament by loving someone according to your vows: for much better or way worse than you imagined, in sickness and in health.

It's relatively easy to do wonderful things for someone when you're receiving all these wonderful things from them in return. But then your husband gets sick, or becomes increasingly distracted or less thoughtful, and he isn't giving you wonderful things with as much enthusiasm and frequency as before. It's at this point that you can learn a lot about yourself. Will I stop giving because I am not receiving, or will I continue to give out of the goodness of my heart—because it is the right thing to do? The unconditionally loving thing to do?

When I found out I was pregnant for the first time, all of a sudden those times when I'd chosen not to give when I wasn't getting hit me square between the eyes. I did a very quick yet thorough inventory of my behavior and considered that another precious soul, a human being, was going to be looking to me to help form and shape him or her into a happy, holy human.

Oh, crap.

I admit: I panicked a bit. When I picked myself up off the floor, I was like, "Uh, dude! We're having a *baby*! We need to get our act toGETHER!" Like an anxious new mom cleaning house before a playdate, I needed to manifest the spiritual fruit of goodness ASAP. It wasn't going to be enough to try to do the right thing for my own sake; I had to cultivate uprightness in my heart and my life for the sake of my growing family.

No. Big. Deal.

Can you sense the sarcasm?

My husband and I were regular Mass attendees, and we really believed that we were on the path to being better people because of our faith; but I couldn't shake the feeling that now, with a baby on the way, there would be someone watching my every move. It was becoming increasingly clear that I had to actually be the kind of person I wanted my children to become.

If I wanted my kids to be kind, patient, and gentle, I would have to be kind, patient, and gentle. There was a very long list of things that I thought I truly *had* to be and do before this little girl arrived. Having grown up pursuing academics and activities, I found a lot of my self-worth in producing, performing, and perfecting. Anything below a "B" in the holiness/saintliness/goodness category was not an option.

And then I remembered, to my chagrin, that although I'd made a U-turn, had a tune-up, and was following my map, I am still a sinner. A big-time sinner. Who was I trying to fool? There was no way I was ever going to be holy enough to be the mom my child needed. The gifts I would bring to the motherhood party weren't going to do me or my kids any favors; I would never be good enough for the precious and innocent souls God was entrusting to my care. I should just pack my bags and hit the road.

Only there was no turning around. This was happening. It wasn't an option. Our current circumstance was the result of the love between my husband and me being blessed by God and exploding into a new human soul. This was a tremendous gift. This was LIFE.

But I had a broken sense of how I should be, because I had a broken sense of how *God* wanted me to be.

God wasn't asking me to be anything other than Heather. He knew me. He knew my heart, he knew my faults, he knew my sins, he knew my goodness and my beauty. And he, in his infinite wisdom, decided it was good for David and me to have a baby. Just like in the Book of Genesis, he ordained our daughter's life, and then he said: "It is very good" (see Gn 1:31). And I could either get on board with it being good because he said so, or I could get caught in the weeds and think that, somehow, I was on my own with this whole motherhood trip.

I think that's where I went wrong: I thought being a good mom was all about *my* goodness. But really, it is about *his*. He is good, so I follow him. I strive to travel through life in a way that is pleasing to him because I love him. Not because I am always going to get it right, not because I am never going to sin, but because he is good. And he made me. And as that old saying goes, "God don't make junk!"

God wants more than our "good" behavior

Remember the old Christmas tune "Santa Claus Is Coming to Town"? Somewhere, somehow, I picked up the notion that God is like Santa in that song. He sees me when I'm sleeping, and he knows when I'm awake. I'm supposed to be good and I'm not supposed to cry; otherwise, I'll get shafted when it comes time for the delivery of the gifts of grace and virtue and heaven and everything else.

I had the wrong notion that God was keeping tabs on my behavior like some sort of heavy-handed, results-oriented Supreme Accountant, indifferently marking down every naughty thing and every good thing, just like Santa's elves, wondering whether I was being good for goodness' sake.

And here's the deal: I did lots of naughty things. Some of my behavior was not *that* bad, but then I'd beat myself up for messing up even that little bit. I'd figure "what's the point?" and just keep sinning. I've done that with lots of things, and maybe you have, too. Dieting comes to mind. You've stayed on plan, eating fresh fruit and veggies and good carbs and drinking lots of water, and then something snaps, and you eat something off the plan, such as, say, half a bag of chips, and you get super down on yourself and say, well, the heck with it—I already messed up as it is; might as well finish off that half-gallon of ice cream from the freezer.

Or think about that book you're reading with your friends. You lost interest on page 12 and now you're avoiding getting together because you feel like such a loser for not keeping up with the reading schedule.

Or novenas. Don't get me started on how many novenas I've started and failed to finish. Ugh.

Sometimes sin is like that. We fall, and instead of quickly getting up and running to our heavenly Father for forgiveness like little children, we feel ashamed and close in on ourselves. The last thing we think we should do is face our Father, who will undoubtedly be supremely disappointed with us and send us to temporary timeout (purgatory) or permanent timeout (hell).

But take another look at the parable of the prodigal son. The father in this story has every right to be frustrated, angry, and hurt. He has every right to completely disown his ungrateful, wayward son. And yet he doesn't do anything of the sort. And God doesn't do that to us, either. He sees us in our sin, he acknowledges our genuine sorrow and penitence, and he doesn't condemn us. What he does is the most loving thing he can do: He tells us to go *and sin no more*.

Eventually, I began to understand: God doesn't want my good behavior. He wants my heart.

I think that might be why the Pharisees were such a thorn in Jesus' side. Perhaps they started off as men who really loved God and wanted to serve him. But in their weakness, they compiled law after law after law in an effort to stay on the narrow way, and soon began idolizing the laws, thinking they would be saved by them rather than being saved by a loving God who wanted to abide with them. Everything the Pharisees did looked shiny and wonderful on the outside, but inside they were full of wickedness (see Lk 11:39). Rather than keeping their eyes fixed on loving God, the Pharisees fell in love with what they thought following the law "perfectly" said about their own goodness.

God doesn't want us to try to be good just so we can boast about our accomplishments and how good we are. Everything should reflect back to him, because only he is good. And the sooner we get on board with that truth, the more likely we will actually find ourselves pulling in safely to our destination.

So be good for goodness' sake

There have definitely been times when I've sought others' approval of me as a mother by signing up for this volunteer gig or that group project, but my heart wasn't in it. I was not doing good for goodness' sake. I was doing it because I thought I had to, out of duty, guilt, or because I wanted someone's approval.

I guess it boils down to this: what's our motive? Are we

doing the right things and following every last jot and tittle of the law so we can appear to be moral, upstanding citizens, made "good" in the eyes of the world because of all the "good" things we're doing? Or do we strive to do the good because we love God and want to please him?

It reminds me of the Act of Contrition. We say we are sorry for our sins because we fear the pains of hell and of losing heaven, but mostly because we have offended God, who is all good and deserving of all our love. If we are only sorry because we are afraid of punishment, that's called imperfect contrition. We are still forgiven, but it's not ideal. Perfect contrition is when we are sorry for hurting God because he is good and faithful and loving and merciful, and we have offended him whom we should love with all our hearts.

Doing good because we love our good God is the more perfected way to roll.

Now I want to have a little heart-to-heart with my fellow rule-followers out there. There's nothing inherently wrong with rules, and there's nothing wrong with following moral rules and laws. For example, the Ten Commandments are nonnegotiable. And the greatest commandment, about loving God and neighbor, is definitely a must-do.

But there are so many ways to be a righteous, upright, and good Christian parent. Truly. G. K. Chesterton talked about the Catholic faith being like a fenced playground. Yes, there are rules, but within that playground, there are so many different options.

We have to be careful that we don't limit God's goodness by saying that holiness and goodness must look like *a, b, c,* or *d.* That's a mistake. Goodness can look as different as there are people on the planet. It's God's goodness, shining through our desire to be upright for his sake.

So for my homeschooling mamas, *you are good.* For the public school mamas, *you are good, too.* For the Catholic or private school moms, *it's all good.* Breastfeeding your baby? *Awesome.* Formula feeding? *Wonderful.* Combo? *Mama, keep up the good work.* Do you stay at home? Do you work from home? Do you work outside the home? Do you work only when you need to? Do you run 5Ks or bake sales or after your kids? Repeat after me: it is *all* good.

For all my prodigal people: do some research on all the crazy ways some of the saints were living before they gave their lives to the Lord, and *then* tell me that he can't use you! My goodness. What are you thinking? Here's a prime example from Saint Francis of Assisi: "I have been all things unholy. If God can work through me, then he can work through anyone."

My friends, God isn't nearly finished with me or my kids yet, and I am pretty sure he isn't finished with you or yours, either. But don't worry. It's all good. If we rely on the Lord, trusting in *his* goodness, the Holy Spirit can help us yield a mighty harvest of good fruit.

Repeat after me: God is good all the time, and all the time God is good. Amen!

● ● ●

Roadblocks to goodness

Sin: When we turn away from God through our sinful behavior, our intellect is darkened and our will is weakened. This makes it much more difficult for us to choose to do the good we know we should do. Whenever we fall, we should quickly seek the Lord's forgiveness, and go to confession as often as necessary.

Perfectionism: You might have heard a version of this phrase, attributed to French writer Voltaire, "The perfect is the enemy of the good." Some of us struggle with wanting things to be just *so*, and when they aren't going exactly according to our plans, we can get overwhelmed and tempted to throw in the towel altogether. It can be easy to lose sight of the good we could be doing while we're hyper-focused on getting everything exactly perfect. As author Father Jacques Philippe said at a recent retreat: let's focus on the good we can do here and now and leave perfection to God.

Rigid adherence to rules: Like the Pharisees of old, some of us can be more interested in crossing every *t* and dotting every *i* rather than focusing on the end result of our efforts to improve our families and communities. While rules are obviously important and deserve respect, let's ask the Holy Spirit to help us keep our focus on the destination itself rather than the precise mode of transportation.

• • •

Yield to the power of the Holy Spirit

(prayer)

Dear Jesus,
Thank you for your infinite goodness and everlasting mercy. I know that every blessing, every good thing comes from your omnipotent hand. Thank you for the tremendous blessing of being a mother. When I fall, help me reconcile quickly with you. May I always, by your grace, bear your image to my children, for you alone are truly good.

Come, Holy Spirit—fill me with your goodness. Amen.

• • •

GPS: God Positioning System

(scripture)

"O how abundant is your goodness,
which you have laid up for those who fear you,
and wrought for those who take refuge in you,
in the sight of the sons of men!" — Psalms 31:19

"Where sin increased, grace abounded all the more."
— Romans 5:20

"Every good endowment and every perfect gift is from above, coming down from the Father of lights with whom there is no variation or shadow due to change." — James 1:17

"If we say we have no sin, we deceive ourselves, and the truth is not in us. ... If we say we have not sinned, we make him a liar, and his word is not in us." — 1 John 1:8, 10

"So then, as we have opportunity, let us do good to all men, and especially to those who are of the household of faith."
— Galatians 6:10

• • •

Roadside Assistance

(wisdom from the saints and others)

"Hope in his goodness and redouble your confidence in proportion as your troubles increase."
— Saint Margaret Mary Alacoque

"One earns paradise with one's daily tasks."
— Saint Gianna Beretta Molla

"All of us can attain to Christian virtue and holiness, no matter in what condition of life we live and no matter what our life work may be." — Saint Francis de Sales

"Great holiness consists in carrying out the little duties of each moment." — Saint Josemaria Escrivá

"You cannot be half a saint.
You must be a whole saint or no saint at all."
— Saint Thérèse of Lisieux

"We do not go to holy Communion because we are good;
we go to become good." — Saint John Bosco

"I have been all things unholy. If God can work through
me, he can work through anyone." — Saint Francis of Assisi

"[We should] throw ourselves into God as a little drop of
water into the sea, and lose ourselves indeed in the ocean of
divine goodness." — Saint Jane Frances de Chantal

• • •

Pit Stop

(other resources)

- Where's your favorite place to pray? Take a moment there soon and ponder all the good God has done in your life. Thank him for his infinite goodness!

- Many women suffer from feeling they aren't good enough mothers to their children. The truth is, almighty God believes you are *exactly* the mom your kids need. Rather than focusing on your parenting missteps or so-called failures, record some ways, no matter how insignificant they may seem, that highlight where you've succeeded. Find a fun way to celebrate your success.

- Ephesians 5:9 tells us that the fruit of light is found in all that is good and right and true. Chat with a friend, neighbor, or with God in prayer about where you see his light shining through your life as a wife and mother.

• • •

Your Ideas

_____

_____

_____

_____

_____

_____

● ● ●

Discuss Amongst Yourselves
(questions)

1. Consider this quote from Father Jacques Philippe, heard recently during one of his retreats in the Pacific Northwest: "I cannot eradicate evil, but I can do good." What are some things we do in support of our vocation as wives and mothers that are good?

2. When God created the heavens and the earth, he saw that they were good. If God peeked into the home you've created, what would he see that is good?

3. What is one way you'd like to inject a little more of God's goodness into your life this week?

KEEP ON TRUCKIN'

((faithfulness))

"The most remarkable thing about my mother is that for thirty years she served the family nothing but leftovers. The original meal has never been found."

— *Calvin Trillin*

• • •

Confession time: there are moments when I want to run away screaming from my house—away from my children, away from the noise, the responsibilities, all of it—and never look back. In fact, I might have almost done that a time or two. There are moments when I want to go to a pitch-black, quiet corner and rock back and forth in the fetal position, plugging my ears with my fingers and humming to myself. And I might have almost done *that* a time or two as well.

Thankfully, God hasn't accepted my halfhearted attempts to resign my position as Supreme Shuttle Bus Chauffeur for the Renshaw household; and, truthfully, my soul is all the better for this gig with which I've been blessed. This is my path to holiness. I have to continue to run the race, as Saint Paul said. And motherhood is a collection of marathons and sprints, to be sure. It's a very long haul, grueling and fraught with difficulties at every turn. Graces and blessings and wonderful things abound, too, of course, but it's not easy being faithful, especially when we don't see what's around the bend. It's a good thing we have the Holy Spirit as our motor, keeping us faithful, keeping us rolling down the right road even when times are tough.

We get knocked down but we get up again

Many moons ago, David and I had two active little girls and another baby on the way. Finances were tight, but we were keeping our heads above water. I was working part time for a small engineering firm, and my husband was working full time for a nonprofit while trying to launch a Catholic men's conference in his spare time. Even though time and money were at a premium, we continued to press forward, trusting that God would bless our simple efforts to provide for our growing family.

With summer and the men's conference right around the corner, I worked hard to wrap things up at my job before taking a short maternity leave while David planned the final details for his event. In addition to the general busyness of this season, we decided to use some of our tax-return money to replace the moldy carpet in the bedrooms as well as the stained and peeling linoleum in the bathroom and laundry room. We were nesting and exhausted but putting one foot in front of the other by the grace of God.

About two weeks before the conference, things started getting weird at la Casa de Renshaw. First, our lawnmower died. It wasn't old, but it also wasn't new enough to be covered under warranty. We figured we could use a neighbor's until we could afford the repairs. Next, the dishwasher went kaput. We learned it would cost more to fix the old unit than to purchase a new one. While an inconvenience, we just didn't have the money for another appliance. What we did have was running water, dish soap, and four adult-sized hands, so we decided to limp along for a while without a dishwasher.

The next calamity wasn't as easy to work around. One morning, as we were getting ready for the day, David went into the laundry room to get something and let out a yelp that turned into a bellow that turned into a panicked exhortation to HEEEEELLLLP! Apparently, the washing machine had gone bonkers in the night, and there was a huge flood of water covering the freshly laid tile and seeping into the newly installed carpet.

What the heck is going on? we asked ourselves. It was as if we were playing Whac-a-Mole with our household problems. We'd deal with one issue, and another would pop up. It was super frustrating and confounding, but we chalked it up to rotten luck and rolled on down the road.

The Thursday before the men's conference, David went to work as usual. I was off for the weekend already, playing with the girls as much as a nine-months-pregnant mama can "play." We were probably just hanging out in the living room, watching a show, hoping the television wouldn't be the next thing to fritz out. Around 3:00 p.m., David called. I knew right away that something was wrong because of the tone of his voice. "They let me go," he said. "I got fired."

After a moment of stunned silence, I found my voice. "Oh, honey, I'm so sorry," I said.

"Yeah," he responded with a sigh. "Me, too."

I tried to put on my best supportive wife voice as I said, "Well, just come home. Everything will be okay." I had no earthly idea how, given our current circumstances, everything would be okay; but I said it anyway.

After the longest hour of my life, my husband walked through the front door carrying a medium-sized cardboard box. I recognized the items that normally decorated his work space. He put the box down and drew me close. "I'm so sorry," I said again as we held each other.

"Hey," he replied, trying to sound upbeat. "Everything happens for a reason, right? Besides, I have a men's conference to put on. I'm sure it will all work out."

I nodded my head and sighed. It sure seemed as though someone or something was trying to kick the snot out of us and then run us over while we were already down for the count.

The rest of the weekend was a blur. David was gone most of Friday prepping the event space and playing host for the conference speakers while I stayed home with the girls. On Saturday, he was out the door at o'dark thirty and came back dog-tired yet enthusiastic. The conference went off without a hitch, thanks be to God, and David received really positive feedback from the attendees. While completely spent from running around like a chicken with his head cut off all day, he seemed at peace and fell asleep the moment his head hit the pillow. I, on the other hand, was exhausted from caring for two active girlies while growing another human being inside my hugely pregnant body while trying to conjure optimism about our financial future inside my brain. I was awake for a while. Sunday was Father's Day, so we went to Mass, ate a yummy brunch at home to celebrate, and spent the rest of the day decompressing from all that had transpired over the past few weeks.

Early Monday morning, I got ready for work and hugged David and the girls goodbye. As I walked out the door, he smiled and reassured me that everything would be fine, that he'd scour the job boards while the girls napped. He was sure he'd find something soon. I prayed and prayed and prayed that he was right. When I arrived home late that afternoon, the girls were playing in the living room and David was sitting at the kitchen table, leaning his head on his right hand, elbow on the table. He looked up at me as I walked in the room, smiling weakly. Having spent time solo parenting both girls recently, I knew he must be tired, but there was something else going on. I began to think perhaps the adrenaline from the men's conference was wearing off and the gravity of our situation had finally hit.

Miraculously, both girls went to sleep right after dinner, so David and I headed back to the kitchen to talk. We sat quietly at the table for a while, each preoccupied with various thoughts and worries. Finally, David spoke. He talked about our bills, and the mortgage, and the broken appliances, and the flood, and the dearth of solid employment opportunities, and then he looked at me in all my massive, pregnant glory, and tears welled in his eyes. He started to say something else but couldn't continue. I had never seen my husband look as dejected and despondent as he did in that moment.

I may never understand exactly what happened next, or why it happened, but suddenly, I stood up, walked over to my husband, looked him in the eyes and shook him by the shoulders. "Peter!" I said, in an uncharacteristically assertive and elevated voice. "Peter! Look at Jesus, not at the waves! LOOK! AT! JESUS!" I let go of his shoulders, since I'd been shaking them the whole time, for emphasis, I guess. I think I sort of shocked both of us. But I kept looking at David, and he kept looking at me. And then the floodgates burst. We started laughing and laughing and couldn't stop. We worried we'd wake up the girls or that I'd go into labor; mercifully, neither of those things happened.

We were reminded, in that moment, that our faith was what mattered. Our family was what mattered. We were going to continue to trust God to provide for us as he said he would, no matter what.

And on June 24, the feast of Saint John the Baptist, as one crying out in the wilderness, our first son was born. We named him Noah, after God's servant who, through his steadfast obedience, helped usher in a new beginning for life on earth. Though he sailed through many deep and difficult waters, Noah trusted that the God of Abraham, Isaac, and Jacob would never forsake or abandon him. Soon enough, a rainbow—the sign of God's promise—adorned the sky.

Just keep swimming ...

Once, when I was going through another particularly stressful time, my friend Wendy preached some truth about God's faithfulness that convicted me down to my soul. She referred to the well-known story "Footprints in the Sand." In this story, a man sees sets of footprints in the sand on a seashore and knows they represent his life. At some points there are two sets of prints, and he recognizes that God was walking with him during those times in his life. At other points, however, he sees only one set of footprints. He wonders where God went during those times. The Lord tells the man that, not only did he not abandon him during these most difficult moments—he *carried* him. The solo footprints belong to Jesus.

Wendy told me that I needed to take a good look at the sandy beaches of my life experiences in the past. "Look at those footprints," she said. "Has God ever dropped you?" she asked. "Has he ever, one time, in your whole life, dropped you?" And then she answered her own question (I love this woman). She said, "No. No, he has never dropped you." She continued, "It could be that he is throwing you around a little bit, like dads sometimes do, but he will never, ever drop you. He never has in the past, and he never will."

And the same goes for you, friend. Life gets hard. Crazy hard. Things happen. Jobs are lost. Children get sick. Natural disasters happen. Adolescents are, well, adolescents. But God Almighty, who began a good work in you, will see it through to completion, come what may. Just keep going. Even if you can't see the end of the road. Even if you're not sure. Just keep on keepin' on, one Glory Be at a time. That's all it takes.

The power of a faithful mom

It has been said that there is no greater gift we can give our children than the gift of faith. And I wholeheartedly agree. Without faith, what's the point? I'm so utterly grateful to my parents for planting the seed of faith at my baptism.

Right now, I want to bring some hope to those of you whose children are older, perhaps, and you're not sure if they are still on board with Jesus, let alone practicing their Catholic faith. Scripture says, "Train up a child in the way he should go, and when he is old he will not depart from it" (Prv 22:6). Sometimes it takes a long time, but remain steadfast in your prayers for your children. Do not grow weary or despair. God is faithful; he is working even if you can't see it today, or even tomorrow.

During my tumultuous adolescence and young adulthood, I had a difficult relationship with my mom. The thing is, though, no matter how angry I was with my her, or how much I railed against her authority and the rules of the house, no matter how bad things got between us, I knew one thing for sure: my mom prayed for me. Without fail. I wasn't even sure if I believed in God anymore, but I knew my mom loved me enough to pray for me. And there is power, sisters, in the prayer of a mother.

Just ask Saint Monica, mother of notorious bad boy-turned-Doctor of the Church Saint Augustine. Or Saint Rita. Or Saint Gianna Beretta Molla. Or the Blessed Mother, who suffered with her Son at the foot of the cross, yet never lost her faith. Pretty much any mother you'd ever want to emulate does one thing for her children: she prays.

And while I'm no saint, thanks be to God and the faithful prayers of my mom and dad and others, I'm back in the fold, a ring on my finger and flip-flops on my feet. We never did kill a fatted calf or have a dance party when I returned; maybe we'll have to schedule that sometime soon.

Fast forward to present day, and it's closing in on twenty years since I returned to the Faith of my youth. I'm a practicing Catholic trying my darndest to raise our children in the Faith. I am the result of a mother's faith and steadfast prayers.

A mother's prayers are powerful. Please don't ever doubt their efficacy at the throne of grace.

We gotta have faith

As I was coming back to the Church, it amazed me to realize

that God had been there all along, waiting for me to return. Even when I wasn't faithful to him, he was faithful to me. All I had to do was turn around, and there he was. When I began to walk toward him, he ran to me and met me where I was, in my filth and in my shame. He had been knocking at the door of my heart all along, yet the only way he would come in was if I invited him, since there was no door handle on his side.

Realizing God's steadfast faithfulness to me, I longed to repay his kindness and his mercy by being faithful in return. I went to Mass at least once a week, went to confession, and endeavored to align my will more closely with his and the teachings of the Church and magisterial authority. This road to faithfulness wasn't without bumps; I had to take a hard look at some of the things I believed about free will and choice, especially with regard to being open to life. While I didn't believe in abortion, I struggled with the Church's teaching on family planning, mostly because I didn't understand it at first.

A friend told me about a homily her pastor gave about Jesus calling his first disciples to radical trust and obedience. After sitting in Simon's boat and preaching to the crowds, Jesus told the fishermen to lower their nets for a catch. Simon protested, "Master, we toiled all night and took nothing" (Lk 5:5). Perhaps Simon and his cohorts scoffed at Jesus' request, thinking, "Who does this guy think he is? He's a carpenter. We've been fishing our whole lives. What does *he* know about catching fish?" Yet despite their doubt, they obeyed. Perhaps they did so begrudgingly; perhaps they did it just to show Jesus that his request was *loco*. Still, they lowered their nets and, unbelievably, pulled in an abundant harvest. Their nets were so full that they were almost to the point of tearing, but they did not break. The homilist drew a connection between the disciples' nets that day and those of us whose "nets" are full because we are open to life. It's possible that God might send more children than we planned for ourselves. While each child is, without exception, a precious gift from God, we can worry that our "net" is already too full, to the point of tearing. But because we are faithful to the Church's teaching, trusting in God's provision, Jesus won't allow our nets to break.

My husband and I have experienced just this. We've welcomed life into our home as God has ordained, at times abstaining to avoid pregnancy. And we've felt like our nets might break. Boy, have we. But they never have. God has always multiplied our love and divided our sorrows. It's just what living in his "upside-down" economy of grace does.

Faithfully following the Church's teachings on natural family planning (or marriage, or abortion, or assisted suicide, or many other countercultural teachings) requires radical trust and obedience. Just like Jesus' disciple, we can't always see what God is doing, but we can trust that he is active in our lives. Whenever I'm having a difficulty with Church teaching, preferring my own understanding or will to the wisdom of Mother Church, I consider those souls who would rather die than be unfaithful to Jesus and the institution he founded. If I am open, the Holy Spirit always finds a way to speak truth to my heart, encouraging me to stay the course like so many holy men and women who went before me.

That's the thing about the great heroes and heroines of the Bible—Mary, Moses, Esther, Paul, Simon Peter—and the saints: they listened to what God asked, no matter how ridiculous it sounded, and then they obeyed. They were faithful.

And I know that, with the Holy Spirit's help, I can be faithful, too.

● ● ●

Roadblocks to faithfulness

Illness and crises: When bad things happen, we can be tempted to wonder where God is in our suffering. The fact is, God never leaves our side, even if we don't feel he is near. When we're going through trials, leaning on the help of our fellow believers can be of great comfort. This is the perfect time to ask friends to lower you down through the roof to Jesus through their prayers and sacrifices. Don't hesitate to beg the Holy Spirit to increase your trust, especially in times of great difficulty. God is faithful. He will do it.

Disappointment: What's one thing you've asked and asked and asked God to do for you, yet it doesn't seem that he has answered your prayer? Through the years, I've learned that God's answer to my requests may be "yes," "no," or "not yet." Trusting that he wants only what is best for us, we can choose to believe that whatever is happening (or not happening) is for our ultimate good. We may ask him to heal our disappointed hearts as we faithfully strive to seek him all the more.

Doubts. Like temptations, doubts are neither here nor there, neither right nor wrong. It is what we do with these doubts that can be virtuous or sinful. Will we stop praying or going to Mass? Or will we seek the Lord where he may be found? When you feel tempted to doubt who God is, what he's promised, or where you're going, ask the Holy Spirit to help increase your faith.

Rebellion (pride): Rebellion springs from disbelieving that God knows what he's doing and is who he says he is. Rebellion says, "I want to do what I want to do when I want to do it. I make the rules. I know better." This sounds a lot like what Lucifer said when he refused to serve God. When we humble ourselves before Almighty God, we understand that he alone is "I AM," the maker of the heavens and the earth. When we surrender our pride and self-seeking agenda, God is faithful to forgive, welcoming us back into his loving arms.

● ● ●

Yield to the power of the Holy Spirit
(prayer)

Dear God,
You have been so faithful to me. Even when I can't see you,
I know that you are always here with me. Give me the faith
to trust that you will never forsake me as I travel through
this valley of tears. Help me to continue to fight the good
fight of faith in good times and bad, realizing that, as long
as I walk with you, all will be well. When I fall, give me
the strength to get up and follow you once more. Heavenly
Father, I believe I can be the Christian, wife, and mother
you've created me to be. Please send your Holy Spirit to help
my unbelief.

Come, Holy Spirit—fill me with your faithfulness. Amen.

● ● ●

GPS: God Positioning System
(scripture)

"Do you not know that in a race all the runners compete,
but only one receives the prize? So run that you may obtain
it." — 1 Corinthians 9:24

"Though a host encamp against me,
my heart does not fear;
though war be waged against me,
yet I will be confident." — Psalms 27:3

"Loyalty and faithfulness preserve the king
and his throne is upheld by righteousness."
— Proverbs 20:28

"Now faith is the assurance of things hoped for, the convic-
tion of things not seen. ... And without faith it is impossible

to please [God]. For whoever would draw near to God must
believe that he exists and that he rewards those who seek
him." — Hebrews 11:1, 6

"Do not let your hearts be troubled. You have faith in God;
have faith also in me." — John 14:1, NABRE

"But he who endures to the end will be saved."
— Matthew 24:13

"The steadfast love of the LORD never ceases,
his mercies never come to an end;
they are new every morning;
great is your faithfulness." — Lamentations 3:22–23

"I believe; help my unbelief!" — Mark 9:24

• • •

Roadside Assistance

(wisdom from the saints and others)

"Many people begin but few finish. And we who are trying
to behave as God's children, have to be among those few."
— Saint Josemaria Escrivá

"Hold your eyes on God and leave the doing to him. That is
all the doing you have to worry about."
— Saint Jeanne de Chantal

"Father, I am seeking: I am hesitant and uncertain, but will
you, O God, watch over each step of mine and guide me."
— Saint Augustine

"Faith is one foot on the ground, one foot in the air, and a
queasy feeling in the stomach." — Mother Angelica

"It is not the actual physical exertion that counts toward a man's progress, nor the nature of the task, but the spirit of faith with which it is undertaken."
— Saint Francis Xavier

"Pray, hope, and don't worry. Worry is useless. God is merciful and will hear your prayer." — Saint Padre Pio

"It's your [domestic] church, Lord. I'm going to bed."
— paraphrase of Pope Saint John XXIII

● ● ●

Pit Stop
(other resources)

- Make an act of faith. Go to a church or to adoration and kneel before the Blessed Sacrament and pray (aloud, if possible), "My Lord and my God." Spend some time with your Savior.

- Revisit the old "Footprints" story. Consider all the times that God has carried you.

- Make an effort to record those times when the Lord has helped you in a journal or diary. Keep it handy so you can read your entries whenever you need a reminder of God's faithfulness in your life.

● ● ●

Your Ideas

_____

_____

_____

_____

_____

• • •

Discuss Amongst Yourselves

(questions)

1. Have you ever hesitated to follow Jesus when times
    were tough? How might you strengthen your resolve
    to choose to follow him even when you don't feel like
    doing so?

2. Think of a time when God really came through for you
    and your family. How did this situation increase your
    trust in him?

3. What are the biggest roadblocks to increasing your
    faith? What is one choice you can make this week to
    help you be more faithful?

AFTERBURNER

((epilogue))

"In the end, I'm the only one who can give my children a happy mother who loves life."
— *Janene Wolsey Baadsgard*

● ● ●

As I write this, I'm sitting in ... wait for it ... *my minivan.* I'm waiting for my eldest daughter to get out of school so we can pick up my youngest son from a play date and then rush to get the three middle children who are about thirty minutes away. The problem is, I forgot the middles had early release from school today. Never mind that they've had early release every Wednesday for the past, oh, nine months straight. I just ... forgot.

Sigh.

I have an alarm set on my phone about early pickup, but I didn't see it. I just worked right through it.

And I forgot them.

My eldest daughter chastised me when she learned of my faux pas: "MOM!" she exclaimed. "What is *wrong* with you?! Why did you forget the kids?!" *Such a good question.*

Here's the thing: recently, I was diagnosed with attention deficit hyperactivity disorder, to add to previous diag-

203

noses of chronic depression and anxiety. While, thanks be to God, the depression and anxiety are under control, the ADHD remains a wild card. I'm not sure if it's just become more pronounced in adulthood, but I have always struggled with staying focused, remembering things, and following through, especially when I'm stressed. And there's nothing like adding incredibly tight work deadlines to the general crazy known as end-of-school-year events to stress a mama out.

Previous iterations of me would have flipped out at my forgetfulness. I would have silently (or perhaps not-so-silently) berated myself with a litany of negative statements about what a horrible person I am, how I'm the world's worst mom, and on and on ad nauseam. I would have spiraled into a funk so fast it would give Danica Patrick a run for her money.

But a funny thing happened not too long ago. I took a turn from my normal route so I could start taking better care of my kids' mom. I saw a counselor. And a psychologist. I began seeing the difference that more water, more sleep, and more physical activity made in my life. I also met with a spiritual director for regular confession, and I went to adoration, and started seeing the fruits of taking care of my soul, too. I stopped saying "yes" to innumerable things that, before, would have driven me to panic attacks, things I agreed to only for fear of letting down someone whose last name was not Renshaw.

Now, none of these fixes are magic bullets; I haven't morphed into an award-winning wife and mother, but I'm learning to live out the "as yourself" part of that verse in Scripture that tells us how to love. I'm more accepting of the me I am today, while working on the me God wants me to be.

The impetus for all this growth was when I decided to pull my minivan off at the road sign that read "Scripture Study: Straight Ahead" a few years back. I began taking that route every day. And soon I was studying God's Word and writing about it and immersing myself in its truths. I was, you might say, fueling up with the Word. It truly became living and effective in my life and, by extension, my vocation. It helped me know more about who God is and who I am. It was also likely the reason I was inspired to write this book.

And the more I know and accept who God is and my identity in him, the more centered I am. More accepting. More able to forgive myself and allow myself a modicum of grace, whereas before I was my own worst critic. I have found that holding myself to ridiculously unattainable standards makes me pretty miserable—and trickles down to my family, too.

You know the Scripture that says, "In Christ I am a new creation," right? Through the prompting of the Holy Spirit, I have begun treating my motherhood more like a job, and I don't mean in a bad way. I try to treat it with the dignity, respect, and awe it deserves. I am helping to shape souls. I am helping my children on their journey to heaven. And that's a huge job; some might say an impossible one. But I'm not fighting it anymore. I'm not dragging my cross behind me. I'm picking it up, embracing it, and following Jesus, one baby step, one Glory Be at a time. That's my job, and my boss is the Lord. And if that means my job description involves a lot of time driving my kids around, so be it. I choose to praise him anyway.

Friends, this old minivan of mine has seen an awful lot of mileage. It's been across the country not once, but twice. It's starting to rattle a bit in places. But you know what? It keeps going, thanks be to God. Just like me. Just like you. And I'm not going to stop driving it because there might be something shinier up ahead. It has been bought at a price. It was paid for. It gets the job done. Just like me. Just like you.

I still don't have this motherhood thing down to a science (see above example about *forgetting my beloved children*). I likely never will get it completely right. But I'm in this for the long haul. I believe that, with the help of the Holy Spirit, I can be the person God is calling me to be in spite of myself. Whenever I veer off course, whenever I need to pull over for a minute, whenever I realize I've taken the wrong exit, God is always there, faithfully waiting to help get me back on track.

After years on the road, this is what I know: God loves me. He won't ever stop loving me. I don't have to do it all, I just need to surrender my agenda and trust in him. So I pick up my cross, and my keys, and my kids (even if I'm late), and I keep my eyes fixed on the horizon—on Christ crucified and resurrected—and on my eternal destination.

And the view, my friends, really isn't all that shabby— not even from a minivan. In fact, it's actually pretty darn amazing.

● ● ●

"May today there be peace within. May you trust God that you are exactly where you are meant to be. May you not forget the infinite possibilities that are born of faith. May you use those gifts that you have received, and pass on the love that has been given to you. May you be content knowing you are a child of God. Let this presence settle into your bones, and allow your soul the freedom to sing, dance, praise, and love. It is there for each and every one of us."

— *Saint Teresa of Ávila*

EUCHARISTEO

((with thanksgiving))

Jesus Christ, my savior, redeemer, and friend — Mere words cannot express how much I need you. Thank you for absolutely *everything*.

Heavenly Father — Thank you for the gift of my life and all my blessings. Thanks for laughing at and with me. I love you so much. Can't wait to hopefully see you someday. After my great-grandkids are born, you willing. Ha, ha!

Holy Spirit — Thank you for being my motor and inspiration! You are quite literally the sacred wind beneath my broken wings. I love you.

Blessed Virgin Mary — Mama, we did it. Thank you for taking this wretched child under your mantle of grace. Thank you for interceding for me and helping me to become more worthy of your Son. *You got next.*

To all the saints and angels who prayed and fought for me and my family during the book-writing process, especially (but not limited to) — Mother Angelica, Saint Francis de Sales, Saint Teresa of Calcutta (my saint-stalker), Saint Thérèse of Lisieux, Saint Michael the Archangel, Saint Elizabeth of the Visitation, and all our overworked and underpaid guardian angels. Thank you!

For my children — Ava, Elise, Noah, Gianna, and Kolbe, without whom I wouldn't be a mother, and would never, ever, ever have purchased a minivan. I love you! Let's go have fun!

To my husband, David — Thank you for helping us get here in the first place. I am grateful for all your sacrifices, both large and small. Love you!

To Mom and Dad — Thank you for choosing to be my parents. Thank you for giving me the gift of faith. Thank you for never giving up on me. I love you.

Bam — I'm so grateful that we are on this motherhood journey together. God was being especially kind when he blessed me with a sister like you. Thank you (and Will) for reading, suggesting, and cheerleading! Love y'all and your kiddos lots!

Nonnie — You always encouraged me to write my little stories and allowed me to pound away on the mint green typewriter in your sewing room for as long as I wanted, even when it was sunny outside. Grandpa, Lola, and Bompa: thank you for your example and your love. May you all rest in peace.

Mom and Dad Renshaw — Thank you for welcoming me into your family with open arms and for allllllll your support with allllllll the things. I am grateful that you're my family! Love you both.

Janet — Thank you for saying "yes" to life despite extremely difficult circumstances. I owe you my life.

May Michael, through the mercy of God, rest in peace.

+++

Christy — I am in awe of your artistic genius! Thank you for taking a chance on my crazy, big dream and capturing the vision for the book cover and icons even better than I could have ever imagined! I love you so much.

The wonderful team at Our Sunday Visitor — Thank you for using your gifts and talents to bring this project to life. God bless you!

Mary Beth, my amazing and gracious editor — Thank you for all your gentle and patient efforts to make this maiden voyage possible! I am so grateful to you.

+++

They say it takes a village; and indeed, without my amazing Village People, none of these words would have been possible.

Renae — You've seen the mess with your own eyes, yet you still want to get coffee with me. Thank you. I love you!

Mary, Cate, Wendy, Rakhi — I almost have no words. You have been there through many ups and downs, and I literally couldn't even without you. I am so very, very blessed that you are my sisters. Thank you, thank you, thank you.

Rebecca — You are all that AND two cups of sauce. Thank you for your insight, friendship, and entrusting me with Rita Lu. Love you to bits.

To the Franciscan Missionary Sisters of Our Lady of Sorrows and the staff at Our Lady of Peace Retreat — Thank you for your ministry. I know it has touched more souls than you can imagine. May your reward in heaven be great!

To my dear sisters at Take Up and Read, especially Elizabeth

Foss, for your steady leadership and vision.

To The Catholic Conspiracy team for allowing a tag-along blogger like me to hang out with the cool kids.

To my *Catholic Sentinel* colleagues, especially Ed, for taking a chance on an unknown columnist and making my "Mea Maxima Cuppa" dreams come true. Thank you so much!

To Ryan, who reminded me to not just talk about it but to be about it. Keep fighting the good fight and writing the good write, my friend.

For Mrs. Sohn, for encouraging me to read as much as I wanted. For Mrs. Beatty in fifth grade, who forbade the use of the word "nice" as an adjective (boring) and the phrase "not to mention," since we obviously were, in fact, mentioning it.

Jaymie, for taking a chance on a weirdo wannabe Catholic writer from the most unchurched area in the nation — Thank you so very much.

Cheryl, for plucking me out of obscurity and telling me I could write — I am forever grateful.

Jon, for being 18.25 percent of the reason this book came to life and for your dope editing skillz — Karaoke soon!

My "It's 3 O'clock Somewhere" sisters — You have been so patient, kind, and encouraging. Truly the Lord has blessed me with amazing sisters in Christ. I want to be like y'all when I grow up! Betsy, Mo, Christy, Kristin — Love you big!

Kate, Maria J., Amber, Marion, Barbara, Laurel, Barb, Sarah, Allison, Liz, Elizabeth, Micaela, Laurel, Bonnie, Gina, Kathryn, Amy, Alisa, Shaina, Christina, Lisa, Katie, Christy,

Danielle, Kaitlyn, Maria F., Betsy, and superhero Emily — Thank you from the bottom of my heart for reading, suggesting, encouraging, and praying. May God bless y'all with his abundant graces! (And I apologize if I forgot anyone … may God reward you!)

Rebecca, Rachel, Blythe, Wendy, and Lauren — Thank you for allowing me to share a smidgen of your wisdom within these pages! Y'all are the best!

Father Jimmy — Thank you for praying for me in my vocation. It is an honor to pray for you in yours.

Father Tim — Thank you for encouraging me to persevere on the path for holiness in spite of myself. You are a gift from God and a glittery blue pen. Thank you.

To Father Michael, Mrs. Funk, Ms. Lisa, all the teachers and staff and the rest of the Visitation community for being so gracious and welcoming to our family.

To my Consecration sisters from Fairhope — Love and miss y'all sooooo much. Dearest Kat, Godmother Angelle, Kathy, Kristin, Eileen, and Stephanie … let's keep praying for one another!

Minal and Wendy — You are unsung heroes. I am so grateful.

Father Flavian (baptism); Father Joseph (confession and communion); Cardinal Levada (confirmation); and Father Jim (matrimony) — Thank you for nurturing my faith with the sacraments.

Sister Miriam James, Sister Ann, Sister Therese, and dear Sister Anne Marie and our family at Our Lady of Peace — Thank you for your prayers and inspiration. I love you all.

Matt Maher, Audrey Assad, and the rest of the cool folks on my writing playlist — Thank you for keeping me on track.

To the folks at the coffee shops, libraries, parking lots, and that one time for an hour in Office Depot who put up with me warming their chairs and stealing their Wi-Fi while I got this done.

To Take Up and Read, the BIS Sisterhood, Catholic Women Rejoice, the Visitation Project, Called to Love, Flourish, Christian Mother's Fellowship, and all the amazing online friends I've met over the years via Twitter, Facebook, and Instagram. Your prayers, encouragement, and support mean the world. Thank you!

And especially to Obi-Wen, my long-suffering spiritual book doula, my trusted sounding board when all hope seemed lost — Your input and contributions are matched only by the generosity of your spirit and the quickness of your wit. Extraordinarily grateful for the coffee line that day at Edel, Wendy. Love you.

Last but not least, to all the mamas out there doing your utmost for God and family — This one's for you. You are not alone, and you are loved beyond measure. God's got you, and he's got this. Y'all are my heroes. If you ever find yourself in my neck of the woods and need some encouragement, a drink, or a nap, let me know. I might be able to help with two-thirds of those things. Email: RealCatholicMom@gmail.com

ABOUT THE AUTHOR

• • •

Heather Renshaw is a wife, mother, speaker, author, and recovering event coordinator. When not ferrying her five children throughout the mission territory of the Pacific Northwest in her overworked minivan (of course), Heather enjoys deep conversations, loud singing, spontaneous dancing, and silent adoration chapels.

She is the author of *Blessed Conversations: The Beatitudes* (2017), and a contributing author to *All Things Girl: Truth for Teens* (2014). Heather's family life column, "Mea Maxima Cuppa," appears in the award-winning *Catholic Sentinel* newspaper each month in the Archdiocese of Portland in Oregon.

Heather's written work has appeared in various online outlets, including Aleteia, CatholicMom.com, and Blessed Is She, as well as in several Take Up & Read publications.

Heather's passion is proclaiming God's greatness at conferences, retreats, via social media, and any other opportunities the Holy Spirit throws her way. She prays all will experience Jesus' great love and Divine Mercy so they can rejoice and be free.

Connect with Heather via Twitter and Instagram (@RealCatholicMom) or her website: www.RealCatholicMom.com.